The Economics and Finance of Cultural Heritage

This book analyses the economic and financial profiles of heritage assets as tourist attractions. Offering both theoretical insights, methods, and global empirical examples, it considers how heritage assets can create economic and social value for a region.

It offers an analysis of micro- and macroeconomic characteristics of heritage assets and their financial management. The importance of innovation in light of technological and market transformations is considered, as well as the sustainable management of heritage assets environmentally and in terms of sustainable tourism. The book delves into the financial assessment of heritage assets with a focus on evaluation models, the technique of project financing and wealth management in the art sector. These topics are illustrated with cases studies of heritage assets managed as tourist attractions to outline successful management strategies. The book draws on examples from a range of sites and locations across Italy, Spain, the United Kingdom, New Zealand, and the United States to show how heritage assets can be an economic stimulus for the development of local economies.

The book will be of interest to academics and students at both undergraduate and postgraduate levels in the fields of tourism economics, cultural studies and environmental studies.

Vincenzo Pacelli, is Aggregate Professor of Banking and Finance at the University of Foggia, Italy, where he teaches a course on the Economics of Financial Markets. He obtained a PhD in Banking and Finance from the University of Rome, La Sapienza, Italy.

Edgardo Sica is Aggregate Professor of Economics at the University of Foggia, Italy. He obtained a PhD in Technology and Innovation Management at the SPRU, UK. His main research interest lies at the intersection of sustainability, innovation, and tourism economics.

Routledge Cultural Heritage and Tourism Series
Series editor: Dallen J. Timothy, *Arizona State University, USA*

The Routledge Cultural Heritage and Tourism Series offers an interdisciplinary social science forum for original, innovative and cutting-edge research about all aspects of cultural heritage-based tourism. This series encourages new and theoretical perspectives and showcases ground-breaking work that reflects the dynamism and vibrancy of heritage, tourism and cultural studies. It aims to foster discussions about both tangible and intangible heritages, and all of their management, conservation, interpretation, political, conflict, consumption and identity challenges, opportunities and implications. This series interprets heritage broadly and caters to the needs of upper-level students, academic researchers, and policy makers.

Heritage of Death
Landscapes of Emotion, Memory and Practice
Edited by Mattias Frihammar and Helaine Silverman

Industrial Heritage and Regional Identities
Edited by Christian Wicke, Stefan Berger and Jana Golombek

Deconstructing Eurocentric tourism and Heritage Narratives in Mexican American Communities
Juan de Oñate as a West Texas Icon
Frank G. Perez and Carlos F. Ortega

Creating Heritage
Unrecognised Pasts and Rejected Futures
Edited by Thomas Carter, David C. Harvey, Roy Jones, and Iain J.M. Robertson

The Economics and Finance of Cultural Heritage
How to Make Tourist Attractions a Regional Economic Resource
Vincenzo Pacelli and Edgardo Sica

For more information about this series, please visit: www.routledge.com/ Routledge-Cultural-Heritage-and-Tourism-Series/book-series/RCHT

The Economics and Finance of Cultural Heritage

How to Make Tourist Attractions
a Regional Economic Resource

Vincenzo Pacelli and Edgardo Sica

Routledge
Taylor & Francis Group

LONDON AND NEW YORK

First published 2021
by Routledge
2 Park Square, Milton Park, Abingdon, Oxon OX14 4RN

and by Routledge
605 Third Avenue, New York, NY 10017

First issued in paperback 2022

Routledge is an imprint of the Taylor & Francis Group, an informa business

Publisher's Note
The publisher has gone to great lengths to ensure the quality of this reprint but points out that some imperfections in the original copies may be apparent.

British Library Cataloguing-in-Publication Data
A catalogue record for this book is available from the British Library

Library of Congress Cataloging-in-Publication Data
A catalog record has been requested for this book

ISBN 13: 978-0-367-52444-9 (pbk)
ISBN 13: 978-0-367-89475-7 (hbk)
ISBN 13: 978-1-003-01939-8 (ebk)

DOI: 10.4324/9781003019398

Typeset in Times New Roman
by Newgen Publishing UK

Contents

Illustrations

Figures

Tables

Introduction

Cultural heritage describes an extremely dynamic and constantly expanding set of assets characterised by strong and expressive aesthetics. The notion was first formalised in 1960s Italy by the Franceschini Commission to represent important assets of civilization, history and culture that, by virtue of their recognised artistic value, belong to the community and are enhanced and protected, accordingly. Today, cultural heritage in Italy is governed by Legislative Decree No. 42 of 22 January 2004, which defines it as the entirety of cultural and landscape assets. In fact, cultural heritage includes not only objects of art and historical value (i.e. documents, books, etc.) but also environmental assets, such as natural or man-made landscapes, that provide evidence of civilization. Due to the heterogeneous nature of cultural heritage assets, in 2009, UNESCO classified these items into six domains, distinguishing between: (i) museums, archaeological sites, monuments and natural landscapes; (ii) performing arts; (iii) visual arts and crafts; (iv) books, newspapers and magazines; (v) radio, television, film and video games; and (vi) fashion, architecture, advertising and design. In this book, specific reference will be made to heritage assets in the first domain – that is, cultural and landscape assets – and, specifically, tourist attractions. Cultural tourism is a strategic resource for Italy, which enjoys a tremendous number of heritage assets in the form of museums, archaeological sites, environmental assets, national parks and marine areas; thus, the combination of culture and tourism is a competitive asset for the national tourism system. To avoid the paradox of abundance, Italy should – with foresight and determination – develop a long-term industrial policy based on the sustainable valorisation in tourist terms of its extraordinary environmental, artistic and cultural heritage; subsequently, this policy should be carried out by precise and courageous political decisions at the national and local levels, supported by adequate investment, in order to trigger virtuous and lasting multiplicative mechanisms of income and wealth.

The present book analyses the economic, financial and management profiles of heritage assets that can also be considered tourist attractions. Chapters 1-4 focus on, from a purely theoretical point of view, the micro- and macroeconomic characteristics of heritage assets and examines the topics of financing and assessment. In Chapters 5–7, national and international cases of heritage assets as tourist attractions are described, through an empirical approach. In this part, the focus is on the management models used by the tourist attractions to become economic drivers for local area, i.e. how they create economic and social value for their region, and not only for the private entities that manage them.

In particular, Chapter 1 analyses the economic dimension of heritage assets, in terms of both related business activities and attempts to make these assets more economically productive, i.e. greater sources of income. This valorisation process should not be conceived in terms of commodification but instead as a way to conserve assets due to the income they generate. The chapter continues with an analysis of the micro- and macroeconomic profiles of heritage assets. From a microeconomic perspective, the need to separate cultural and landscape assets from their value as tourist attractions is particularly evident, since each of these aspects requires a different theoretical approach. The macroeconomic analysis, on the other hand, focuses on the complexity of defining the heritage asset sector, identifying its performance indicators and determining the multiplier effects that heritage assets can determine on the local economy.

Chapter 2 focuses on two of the performance indicators identified in Chapter 1: innovation and environmental sustainability. The importance of innovation lies mainly in the opportunities to expand the tourist use of heritage assets in light of technological and market transformations. Innovation also entails new skills and, consequently, new training needs, with extremely positive effects in terms of employment. The analysis focuses on technological innovation and digitisation – both of which are particularly relevant for the heritage asset sector as they offer significant opportunities for modernisation. The issue of sustainability, on the other hand, relates to the sustainable management of cultural heritage, recognising the positive externalities it can generate. The analysis focuses in particular on the environmental sustainability of heritage assets, first in their general meaning as cultural and landscape assets – in terms of energy savings and use of renewable sources – and then in their specific role of tourist attractions – in terms of sustainable tourism and load capacity.

Chapter 3 explores the issues of heritage asset financing and wealth management in the arts sector. In particular, project financing is examined in depth, as this technique is considered particularly useful and suitable for cultural and environmental heritage financing due to the medium size of the necessary funds, the complexity of the operations and the often mixed body of public and private stakeholders. It then turns to the issue of strategic, economic and financial planning, through an analysis of business plan management, which is considered an essential tool for the public and private financing of heritage assets. After analysing the main opportunities for the public financing of heritage assets in Italy and Europe and raising some critical considerations over European and Italian gaps in the coordination and strategic planning of investment policies for cultural and environmental heritage, the chapter concludes by examining the management of assets invested in art and the development of financial services related to the art world.

Chapter 4 deals with the complex and controversial issue of the valuation of heritage assets as economic assets capable of generating income given appropriate investment in their management, protection and conservation. While the process of estimation determines the value of a cultural or landscape good, the mechanisms of competition and negotiation determine its price. Often, the value and price of a cultural or landscape good do not coincide. For this reason, Chapter 4 initially examines the difference between the price and value of a cultural and landscape asset and then outlines the main methodologies used to value such heritage assets. In this respect, it should be noted that the value of a culture or landscape good is not only economic but also social and cultural; therefore, its value – or 'sensual side' – is difficult to measure. Moreover, the cultural or social benefits it can generate for the community are difficult to quantify from an economic point of view and not necessarily quantitatively identified in the value or price of the asset considered. Notwithstanding these challenges, it seems safe to assume that a public or private entity would be motivated to invest in a given cultural or landscape asset (to secure its protection, preservation or enhancement) as long as the asset is at least potentially able to generate some benefit (economic, social, scientific or cultural) for its shareholders or stakeholders. It is therefore clear that the assessment of heritage assets, while complex and slippery, is of absolute importance for a multitude of subjects, such as public contributors, local residents, public or private investors or administrators of the public or private entities.

Chapter 4 concludes the first – purely theoretical – part of the book. The second part opens with Chapter 5, which deals with the empirical analysis of case studies. The case study methodology has the dual purpose of conveying both the main connotations of the phenomena under analysis and the dynamics of a given process. The qualitative approach thus allows to describe, explain and provide insight into situations and phenomena in terms of their dynamics and evolution.

Following this methodological approach, Chapter 5 analyses caves as an environmental and tourist resource, first describing the general state of play of Italian caves and then exploring the specific cases of the Waitomo Glowworm Caves in New Zealand and the Castellana Caves in Italy. Speleological tourism (i.e. tourism linked to caves), has recently become a valuable economic resource for many areas – and particularly Italy, which boasts a large number of natural cavities equipped for tourism. It is estimated that Italian tourist caves are visited by more than 1.5 million persons each year, generating an aggregate annual turnover of approximately 20 million euros. The chapter also considers services related to cave visits, such as speleological museums, bookshops and photo and gadget vendors in the cave vicinity. When these related services are considered, as well as local catering services, accommodation facilities, commercial activities and sports venues, the annual turnover of the caves tends to double. In this way, tourist caves that are properly exploited can support collateral activities (e.g. services and accommodation), provide employment opportunities and attract public and private investment, thereby feeding a virtuous cycle with multiplier effects on local production and income.

Chapter 6 examines the contribution of cultural tourism flows generated by museums to local development, in light of the recent reorganisation of the Italian museum system. To this end, the chapter analyses three very different cases in terms of governance model, geographical location and socio-economic context: the Pinacoteca di Brera, the National Archaeological Museum of Taranto (MArTA) and the RavennAntica Foundation (responsible for managing part of the cultural heritage of the municipality of Ravenna, including some museums). The survey considers management aspects of the three cases, including their strategic objectives and commercial development and promotion strategies, as well as the results they have achieved from these strategies. Information collected are then cross-referenced with statistical data from external sources to show how each of the three cases conceives cultural tourism and exploits its potential to generate a positive impact on the local economy.

The seventh and final chapter analyses a series of European and US cases of successful heritage asset management – particularly with regard to the generation of economic and social value for the local community. The overview begins at the Guggenheim Museum in Bilbao – an extraordinary architectural, cultural and economic operation that has radically changed the face and economy of the Spanish city. The Serralves Foundation, located in the nearby city of Porto, is much less well known than the Basque museum. Since its inception, it has set itself the goal of maintaining constant dialogue with the city and creating a supportive community base. The third case is that of National Museums Liverpool – a single body comprising eight different museums, all with free admission; two-thirds of the funding for this organisation is provided by the UK government, but it is now seeking new sources of livelihood. These European cases are succeeded by an Italian case from a region neighbouring a German-speaking territory: the Merano Thermal Baths, which are more than 99% owned by the Autonomous Province of Bolzano. The chapter then concludes with two US cases. The first is of Balboa Park in San Diego, California – a complex and articulated collection of dozens of museums, institutions and businesses – and the second is of the Museum of Fine Arts in Boston, Massachusetts – the fifth largest museum complex in the United States, and one of the oldest.

This book was jointly conceived and produced by the two authors. However, Chapters 3, 4, 5 and 7 were written by Vincenzo Pacelli, while Chapters 1, 2 and 6 by Edgardo Sica. Introduction was jointly written by the two authors.

1 Micro- and macroeconomic characteristics of heritage assets

Heritage assets among culture, landscape and tourism

The notion of cultural heritage was first introduced in Italy by the Commission of Inquiry for the Protection and Enhancement of the Historical, Archaeological, Artistic and Landscape Heritage (i.e. the 'Franceschini Commission'), established by the Ministry of Education's Law No. 310 of 26 April 1964. The Commission defined cultural heritage as the set of all important assets of civilisation, history and culture that, by virtue of their recognised artistic value, belong to the community, represent history and are the object of aesthetic education; for this reason, such objects are considered worthy of enhancement and protection. It is clear from this definition that cultural heritage is not only identifiable with objects of art, but it also includes everything of historical value, including documents, books, materials, artistic and expressive experiments and everyday objects. Furthermore, it includes environmental assets, such as natural or man-made landscapes, that provide evidence of civilisation.

Cultural heritage assets may be 'tangible' or 'intangible'. Tangible assets have a defined and stable form, and include paintings, statues, architecture and archaeological artefacts. Intangible assets, in contrast, exist only in the moments in which they are enacted, and include festivals, popular performances, processions, religious rites, sporting events and competitions. Furthermore, cultural heritage assets can be 'mobile' or 'immovable'. The former can be transported from one place to another without their integrity being compromised (e.g. paintings, sculptures, coins, etc.), while the latter are permanently anchored to a particular place (e.g. frescoes, monuments, archaeological sites, landscape assets, etc.). As far as environmental assets are concerned, these can be traced back to 'individual' beauties (i.e. those that preserve an uncommon intrinsic spontaneous value, such as parks, caves, natural bays, etc.) or to 'whole' beauties, such as natural forms or buildings that form an integral part of a unitary complex of particular value.

Cultural heritage is now governed by the Code of Cultural Heritage and Landscape (Legislative Decree No. 42 of 22 January 2004), which defines it as the set of all cultural and landscape assets (Art. 2). The Code also provides a precise definition of each of the two types of goods, also establishing the constraints to which they are subject and the actions made to protect and safeguard them.

According to the code, cultural assets are: 'immovable and movable assets which [...] are of artistic, historical, archaeological, ethnoanthropological, archival and bibliographic interest and other assets identified by law or by law as having the value of a civilisation' (Art. 2). Such goods include: 'collections of museums, art galleries, galleries and other exhibition sites [...] archives [...] book collections [...] of the State, the regions, other local authorities [...]', as well as those belonging to private entities. Among other things, cultural assets are also 'books [...] musical scores [...] photographs [...] films [...]', provided they are 'rare and valuable', and 'villas, parks and gardens [...] public squares, streets, streets [...]', provided they have 'artistic or historical interest' (Art. 10).

Landscape assets, on the other hand, are 'real estate and areas [...] that are an expression of the historical, cultural, natural, morphological and aesthetic values of the territory, and the other assets identified by law or by law' (Art. 2). These include 'immovable things that have conspicuous characteristics of natural beauty, geological singularity or historical memory, [...] villas, gardens and parks, [...] historical centres and nuclei; [...] panoramic beauties [...], coastal territories [...], rivers, streams, watercourses [...], mountains [...], glaciers [...], parks and reserves [...]' (Arts. 136, 142).

Cultural heritage is therefore a dynamic and ever-expanding set of assets characterised by strong and expressive aesthetics. It expresses the unrepeatable and irreproducible (i.e. unique) values of the society from which it emanates; for this reason, cultural heritage possesses important economic value that, alongside their historical, artistic and cultural value, allows it to constitute an important source of local and national revenue. Due to the high degree of heterogeneity of cultural heritage assets, UNESCO classifies them into six domains (UNESCO, 2009):

- 'cultural and natural heritage', including museums, archaeological sites, monuments, natural and cultural landscapes, and movable and immovable objects of symbolic, historical, artistic, aesthetic, ethno-anthropological, scientific and social value, as well as their related activities;
- 'performance and celebration', including performing arts, festivals, fairs and music-related goods and activities;
- 'visual arts and crafts';
- 'books and presses', including industries active in the production of books, newspapers and magazines;
- 'audio-visual and interactive media', including radio, television and film, video games and everything related to the Internet and computer science; and
- 'design and creative services', including fashion, architecture, advertising and design, in their various meanings.

UNESCO also proposes a transversal domain of 'intangible cultural heritage' (according to the 2003 UNESCO Convention), as well as other related categories, such as tourism, sport and entertainment. It also links education, training, archiving, conservation and use of supporting equipment and materials to these domains.

In the following, specific reference will be made to the domain of 'cultural and natural heritage' – or, more simply, 'heritage assets' – considering, in particular, those with a strong link to tourism. If we consider tourism more than a mere mercantilist contamination that is incompatible with an elitist vision of cultural heritage (Volpe, 2018a), then we may subsequently consider heritage assets to embody the dual value of *cultural and landscape assets* on the one hand and *tourist attractions* on the other. These are, of course, two sides of the same coin and not always possible to separate. However, recognition of the tourist value of heritage assets, in addition to their value as cultural and landscape assets, was formalised in Italy in the Legislative Decree No. 71 of 24 June 2013, which entrusted tourism to the Ministry of Cultural Heritage and Activities, transforming its acronym from MiBAC to MiBACT (Ministry of Cultural Heritage and Activities *and Tourism*).[1] This change in responsibilities aimed at lending a new strategic centrality to cultural heritage; in so doing, it was hoped that heritage assets would obtain more resources for their protection and enhancement and that new employment opportunities for cultural heritage professionals – also in services related to cultural tourism and landscapes – would be created.

According to the UN World Tourism Organization (UNWTO), tourism comprises the set of activities that people engage in outside of their usual environment for at least 24 hours and up to 1 year, for reasons of recreation or pleasure (or any reason other than the pursuit of remuneration) (UNWTO, 2008). Tourism, by nature, is characterised by a marked transversality that makes it difficult to place within the traditional economic classifications of agriculture, industry or services. In fact, it is strongly integrated within each of these activities, other than within cultural heritage.

Within each of these traditional classifications, we can note a strong growth in cultural tourism over recent years. Cultural tourism, in particular, is defined as the set of all movements of people motivated by cultural purposes (e.g. cultural events, visits to archaeological sites and monuments, etc.) that also concerns the pleasure of immersion in a local lifestyle and everything that constitutes its identity and character (UNWTO, 2005). It is, therefore, a form of tourism that is entirely or partially motivated by an interest in the history, art, science, traditions and lifestyles of a particular locality (i.e. its culture).

Cultural tourism is a strategic resource for Italy – a country with one of the largest numbers of heritage assets in the world (more than 3,400 museums, 2,100 archaeological sites and 20 national parks and marine areas). Moreover, 54 Italian sites are recognised as UNESCU World Heritage Sites; this makes Italy the nation with the highest concentration of World Heritage Sites, both in absolute terms (followed by China, with 53 sites, and Spain, with 47) and relative terms (in relation to sites per geographical area). The historical, artistic and landscape heritage of not only Italian cities, but also small urban centres scattered throughout the country, is a unique aspect of Italy, and among the primary factors that motivates the inflow of tourists from overseas. The first five Italian cultural sites listed (the Colosseum, the Excavations of Pompeii, Uffizi Gallery, the Accademia Gallery of Florence and the National Museum of Castel Sant'Angelo), for example recorded more than 15 million visitors in 2017, which corresponds to more than 30% of all visitors to Italian heritage sites (CISET, 2018). The combination of culture and tourism represents the Italian true competitive tourist asset, as also confirmed by the nation's Global Reputation, according to the latest Country Brand Index – one of the major indicators of trends in countries as global brands. The index shows that tourism and cultural experiences are the main components of Italy's attractiveness and recognition (i.e. reputation base).

If Italy's cultural and landscape assets strongly characterise its global image, they also represent the most promising assets of the Italian tourist offer. This is confirmed by CISET data showing that, in the period of 2011–2016, tourist flows in Italian cities of historical and artistic interest significantly increased. Indeed, in 2016, arrivals in these cities amounted to 41,931,069 (35.9% of Italy's total tourist arrivals and +13.4% compared to 2011), whereas the number of presences was 109,691,804 (27.2% of Italy's total tourist presences and +11.6% compared to 2011). In addition, the number of visitors to Italian cultural heritage sites in 2013–2017 grew 31% over the period, from approximately 38 million in 2013 to more than 50 million in 2017, corresponding to a 53% increase in revenue, from more than 80 million euros in 2013 to more than 193 million in 2017 (CISET, 2018).

The recent development of Italy's cultural tourism is undoubtedly linked to the nation's simultaneous increase in education and family income, which has prompted traditional 'consumers of tourist goods' to spend more time and money on trips and experiences involving inner aspects of their personality. However, these factors, alone, are not enough to explain the growth in cultural tourism. In particular, other factors may include: (i) increased desire for an 'authentic' tourist experience that enables tourists to engage with a place's true identity and to come to understand its art, history and traditions; (ii) increased interest in mass-market cultural events that are often strongly advertised in the media; and (iii) holiday fragmentation, with demand for tourism increasingly oriented towards short breaks during the year rather than a single longer holiday. In the latter regard, Italy, in the face of a positive trend in the number of tourist arrivals in the period of 2001–2015 (+50%), recorded a significant decrease in tourists' average length of stay, from 4.1 to 3.6 days in the same period (CISET, 2018).

The economic dimension of heritage assets

Considered both cultural and landscape assets *and* tourist attractions, heritage assets bear an appreciable economic potential. On the one hand, when they are considered merely cultural assets, they represent a productive sector with a potential multiplier effect on the economy. On the other hand, when they are *also* conceived as tourist goods, they significantly contribute to increase the socio-economic benefits.

Thus, from an economic point of view, heritage assets may be thought to provide multiplier effects and employment opportunities; and from a social point of view, they may be thought to increase cultural tourism and thereby increase well-being and education.

In recent years, growing attention has been placed on the economic dimension of heritage assets. For example 2018 was the European Year of Cultural Heritage, emblematic of the importance that the European Commission places on cultural and landscape assets in terms of their ability to create growth and employment and be an engine of economic development in the European Union. Reasons for this growing interest in heritage assets as a flywheel of the economy can be found in both technological innovation (in particular, diffusion of the Internet, which has made a growing amount of information available and increased information demand) and the scarcity of public resources for the protection and enhancement of these assets. The latter has generated a view that private industry should provide financial support for these cultural and landscape assets.

The economic dimension of heritage assets can be defined in terms of 'connected entrepreneurial activities' and 'economic enhancement' (Cozzi, 2018). According to the former, the economic relevance of heritage assets lies in their related business activities, such as tourism and related services, administrative activities aimed at preserving the assets and the cultural industry. On the other hand, the latter assumes that the economic importance of heritage assets lies in their efficient 'economic management', in terms of balancing costs and benefits and generating economic value from the intersection between supply and demand, with resulting multiplier effects on the local context, such as greater demand for related goods and services. The recent data elaborated by CISET show that 2017 demonstrated the highest average expenditure per cultural tourist (Table 1.1), and that the shopping basket of these cultural tourists tended to be more differentiated, on average (Table 1.2).

Table 1.1 Average expenditure of tourists in Italy, 2017, by destination (CISET, 2018)

Type of destination	Average expenditure per tourist (€)	% of total holiday expenditure
Seaside	89.00	20.5
Alpine	96.50	4.8
Lacustrine	77.60	9.3
Cultural	133.00	57.7
Cultural landscape	117.00	7.7
TOTAL (on holiday)	112.00	100

Table 1.2 Shopping basket of cultural tourists (CISET, 2018)

Expenditure items	% of total
Accommodation	37.9
Food/restaurants	16.2
Transport	11.7
Shopping	15.9
Other services	9.8
Other assets	8.5
TOTAL (on holiday)	100

The 'valorisation' of heritage assets refers to the attempt to make these assets productive (i.e. a source of income). This objective can be achieved through the promotion of cultural tourism (i.e. encouraging the use of cultural and landscape assets by promoting them as tourist attractions). Heritage assets can generate a flow of goods and services – each with their own economic and cultural value – for either immediate consumption or the production of further goods and services. In this sense, if heritage assets are protected and conserved, they represent capital assets whose productivity may create externalities that are both cultural and non-cultural, with the latter including externalities linked to social, economic and productive contexts (e.g. tourism, real estate and cultural entrepreneurship) (D'Auria, 2017). It is important to note that the economic enhancement of heritage assets should not be understood as antithetical to the protection and enhancement of cultural heritage; however, it is always subordinate to this aim. If, on the one hand, Article 9 of the Italian Constitution (second paragraph) states that the Republic 'protects the landscape and the historical and artistic heritage of the Nation', the first paragraph, on the other hand, specifies that 'The Republic promotes the development of culture and scientific and technical research'. Therefore, in the Italian Constitution, the protection of heritage assets is linked to the promotion of culture and research (Volpe, 2018b). From this perspective, enhancement of cultural and landscape assets should not be understood as a process that necessarily leads to their commercialisation. On the contrary, the resulting profitability should ideally drive better conservation and use of the assets. The CISET data show that, compared to other forms of tourism (e.g. seaside tourism), cultural tourism demonstrates greater potential for profitability due to cultural tourists' particularly high propensity to spend. The economic importance of heritage assets, therefore, calls for reflection on their micro- and macroeconomic dimensions.

Microeconomic analysis of heritage assets

The present microeconomic analysis of heritage assets considers the dynamics of their supply and demand, their market structure and their possible inefficiencies. However, the findings differ depending on whether the heritage assets are considered 'cultural and landscape assets' or 'tourist attractions', as each of these profiles demands a different type of analysis.

Microeconomic profile of heritage assets as cultural and landscape assets

Considered cultural and landscape assets, heritage assets are subject to protection and enhancement; therefore, they escape a traditional microeconomic analysis. In this context, even the use of microeconomic terminology seems inappropriate in some ways. For example the verb 'to consume' (from the Latin word *consummare*, literally 'to end up little by little with use, to wear out, to exhaust'), when placed alongside 'cultural and landscape assets', seems an oxymoron, because it is associated with the 'wear and tear' of a good (the heritage asset) that, instead, should be – by definition – protected and preserved (see, in this regard, Di Maio and De Simone, 2006). The impossibility of examining cultural and landscape assets using a traditional approach means that the relevant microeconomic aspects are essentially limited to: (i) the characteristics of the demand for such assets and (ii) their nature as public goods.

Individual demand for cultural and landscape assets is positively influenced by consumers' higher disposable income and spending power, as well as their higher level of education. It may also depend on psychological and sociological decisions that are difficult to predict, rather than purely economic choices. Use of heritage assets, in fact, occurs mainly in consideration of the emotions or aesthetic gratification that they produce in the consumer; such aspects easily escape the axioms on which the neoclassical theory of the consumer is based. In this respect, it is possible to identify four types of consumers. The first type is made up of 'highly motivated' individuals, whose main objective is to benefit from a certain heritage asset, in itself (e.g. by visiting a museum or monument). Generally, such consumers have a high level of education and willingness to pay. The second group is made up of 'partially motivated' consumers, who combine the use of heritage assets with an opportunity (e.g. for a trip). The third group is comprised of consumers for whom the cultural and landscape good represents an 'additional motivation' beyond other consumption needs. Finally, the fourth group is represented by consumers who do not plan to use the heritage asset, but visit it only by chance, driven by (generally) non-cultural motivations. Therefore, compared to the neoclassical approach, the theory of random utility (i.e. 'random utility maximisation') seems more effective for modelling demand for cultural and landscape assets, since it considers the utility of a random consumer alongside that of an observable one. The reference theory for this analysis derives from Lancaster (1966), who holds that consumers perceive a good as a vector of characteristics from which they derive satisfaction and to which it is possible to assign specific shadow prices. From this perspective, a heritage asset can be broken down into a set of qualities that make up its aggregate value.

Therefore, the assessment of consumer preferences in the case of cultural and landscape assets should comprise multiple qualitative and quantitative attributes of the goods under consideration, making the measurement of the significance of each individual attribute an explanatory factor of individual demand.

As regards the public goods nature of heritage assets, this represents an important cause of market failure (i.e. whereby the allocation of goods and services is not Pareto efficient). An economic system configuration is Pareto efficient when the well-being of one consumer cannot be improved without worsening that of another. The first fundamental theorem of the economy of well-being has, among its many assumptions, that all goods exchanged in the economic system have a private nature, since private goods are the only ones that can be efficiently exchanged in the market. It should be recalled that a 'pure private good' is characterised by rivalry in consumption and the exclusion of the benefits of its consumption. In this scenario, the consumption of a good by a particular individual prevents the simultaneous consumption of the same good by others, and thus restricts the latter from enjoying the same benefits. This means that consumption of a pure private good imposes an opportunity cost on those who are unable to consume it. On the other hand, with respect to pure private goods, it is possible to exclude those who do not pay from using the good, and therefore from receiving its benefits. In this sense, a pure private good has well-defined property rights whereby the owner can set and enforce the terms by which ownership can be transferred to others.

In contrast, a 'pure public good' is characterised by the non-rivalry of its consumption and the non-excludability of the benefits of its consumption (think, e.g. of the case of public lighting).[2] It follows that, in the case of a pure public good, several individuals can simultaneously benefit from the good without diminishing the utility of the good for others.[3] Furthermore, if the good is available to some person, it is not possible or convenient for that person to exclude others from the benefits the good produces. Finally, within the hypothetical line that joins pure private goods to pure public goods, it is possible to place, at an intermediate level, 'mixed public goods', for which there may be rivalry in consumption, and 'spurious public goods', for which it is instead possible to implement some form of exclusion (Table 1.3). In this framework, heritage assets include pure public goods (e.g. cultural goods of a city of art), spurious public goods (e.g. museums) and mixed public goods

Table 1.3 Classification of public and private goods

	Excludable	*Non-excludable*
Rival	Private goods	Mixed public goods
Non-rival	Spurious public goods (or club)	Pure public goods

(e.g. landscapes), for which rivalry in consumption can intervene due to congestion.

The nature of heritage assets as public goods prevents the determination of an optimal (i.e. Pareto efficient) quantity of such assets within the market. Non-rival and non-excludable consumption of heritage assets as pure public goods leads to market inefficiencies (i.e. failures), since consumers have no incentive to declare the price they would be willing to pay for their consumption. In fact, to obtain a Pareto efficient allocation of a pure public good, each individual consumer should pay the maximum that he is willing to pay for the amount of public good he uses. In this condition, each consumer is likely to pay a different price, and balance will only be achieved if each individual is completely sincere in expressing his true willingness to pay (which is a value known only to the individual). However, no individual would have the advantage of revealing his preferences (i.e. declaring his contribution to the production of the heritage asset, thinking that this contribution, being marginal, cannot influence the quantity produced). In this way, the consumer would leave it to other individuals to declare their willingness to pay, and also to use the good (which is indivisible), without paying (free-riding). Sub-optimal Pareto efficiency is generated even when the heritage asset is considered a spurious or mixed public good. In all these circumstances, therefore, a collective solution is required – or a collective choice mechanism – that entirely replaces individual choice or applies the preferences of select citizens to the larger community. According to value theory, the value of a public good does not depend on the production process (as in non-reproducible goods) or exchange, but on its ability to influence collective well-being. From this perspective, cultural and landscape assets are similar to public goods of collective property and objects of public use, and therefore characterised by their 'value of social use', expressed as a function of collective needs; alternatively, their value may derive from their ability to meet the needs of individuals and, therefore, provide social benefits.

Microeconomic profile of heritage assets as tourist attractions

When considering heritage assets as tourist attractions, analysis shifts to the microeconomic characteristics of cultural tourism in terms of: (i) demand, (ii) supply, (iii) market ownership and (iv) market inefficiencies.

With regard to individual demand, it must be said that, similar to other forms of tourism, cultural tourism is subject to 'towing', 'snobbish' and 'Giffen' effects much more frequently than other goods and services (Delbono and Fiorentini, 1987). First, an increase (decrease) in market demand for a specific cultural destination can increase (reduce) individual demand for that destination (i.e. a towing effect). Second, in the context of very sustained market demand, a consumer may be pushed to replace the demanded cultural destination with a more refined destination (i.e. a snobbish effect). Third, and closely linked to this, individual demand may be subject to a Giffen effect, which increases demand for a cultural destination whose use entails a particularly high consumer price (e.g. additional costs may be incurred when travelling to a location in which there is a popular tourist attraction), but is perceived (for this reason) as distinctive and exclusive. It is obvious that the Giffen effect could combine with the towing or snobbish effects, or, on the contrary, counterbalance them and subsequently cancel them out. Such effects make it impossible to identify the Marshallian market demand for cultural tourism. From a microeconomic perspective, market demand for a good is equivalent to the horizontal sum of individual demand for the good, provided that the quantity of the good purchased by each consumer is not influenced by that which is purchased by others. On the basis of this, such an analysis cannot be applied to cultural destinations, whose individual demand curves escape the assumption of independence.

As regards the supply side, the traditional concept of the production function – understood as the maximum quantity of a product that can be obtained by combining production factors, given a technological constraint – is clearly not applicable. In tourism production, the availability of production factors is usually limited because the inputs into the production process are difficult to reproduce and cannot be the subject of a transaction. In the case of cultural tourism, the inputs are not even reproducible because they are linked to a unique cultural heritage (e.g. a museum) or landscape (e.g. a cave).

The third analytical profile concerns the characteristics of the cultural tourism market, which is particularly varied and, as we will later see, difficult to identify since it consists of a very articulated supply chain that includes everything individuals consume in order to benefit from the heritage asset (ranging from plane tickets to local accommodation). In this framework, it is only possible to analyse the main characteristics of market demand and supply, and it is not possible, as mentioned above, to derive the respective Marshallian curves. Market demand is highly atomised and, in recent decades, it has experienced significant growth at a global level due to the phenomenon of globalisation, which has supported the international flow of tourists, including cultural tourists. In addition, the massive spread of low-cost airlines and the development of the Internet, as mentioned above, have enabled consumers to organise cultural trips in total autonomy. Similar to demand, market supply is also generally atomised, with each country enjoying the presence of numerous heritage assets. These tourist attractions are significantly differentiated, and this differentiation is substantial in nature and not merely formal. Consumers may be willing to bear additional costs linked to, for example a cultural or landscape asset's inconvenient location, since it is perceived as unique or exclusive.

Finally, the cultural tourism market has inefficiencies that do not enable a 'Pareto optimum'. According to the theory of well-being, any configuration of the economic system represents a particular allocation of resources – that is a specific combination of factors used to produce a certain vector of goods and services allocated to different agents within the economic system. According to the first theorem of the welfare economy, any configuration of the economic system resulting from competitive equilibrium is Pareto efficient. Clearly, the existence of information asymmetries undermines the starting hypothesis of this first theorem, thus determining inefficiencies within the market. Cultural and landscape assets are, by definition, 'experience goods', that is assets whose usefulness cannot be fully assessed until they have been used. In this respect, it should be considered that, until approximately 20 years ago, consumers had, *ex ante*, a very limited range of information to guide their decision-making processes around consumption. The existence of information asymmetries threatened, at base, the possibility for consumers to achieve a fully informed tourist choice. However, information asymmetries have been considerably reduced in recent decades, mainly due to the digital revolution that has taken place since the late 1990s as a result of the growth and spread of the Internet. This has led to a total change in consumer behaviour that has affected both planning and use of heritage assets. Today, the number of consumers using search engines as their main source of information on a cultural or landscape asset, to plan and book a cultural holiday online or to create content and share it on social networks is constantly increasing. This has significantly raised the amount, type and quality of information available to consumers, who can now – at the click of a button – easily find descriptions, features and images of tourist attractions they intend to visit and, in many cases, even take a virtual tour of them. In addition, there is widespread use of 'opinion sharing' sites aimed at collecting reviews of a tourist good by those who have already 'experienced' it. In this sense, the TripAdvisor website is emblematic of the way in which digital innovation has significantly reduced the information gap within the tourism market, enabling consumers to make more reasoned choices based on the experiences of others. In other words, the reviews left by other visitors 'signal' the characteristics of the heritage asset, making it easier for intended visitors to decide whether or not they wish to personally benefit from that tourist attraction.[4]

Macroeconomic analysis of heritage assets

Identification of the heritage assets sector

The macroeconomic analysis of heritage assets presents the challenge of identifying the sector of cultural and landscape assets in light of their shared value as tourist attractions. From this perspective, the sector is a complex reality, stratified and with uncertain boundaries and, therefore, difficult to define and delimit because it involves a heterogeneous set of economic activities that cannot be easily aggregated on the basis of traditional criteria (i.e. production mechanisms or product characteristics). The most important consequence of this is that the sector cannot be immediately detected by national accounts data. In order to overcome this problem, we may identify the sector of cultural and landscape assets by considering all of the productive sectors that participate in the offer of goods and services to consumers of heritage assets. This requires the analytical identification of not only all goods and services involved in the direct provisioning of heritage assets, but also all economic activities that – although not directly aimed at satisfying the demand for cultural and landscape goods – directly or indirectly supply the earlier-mentioned sectors. Such an estimation is, understandably, extremely complex.

Alternatively, it is possible to make an estimate based on demand, rather than supply, isolating only that part of the aggregate expenditure aimed at satisfying the needs for consumers of cultural and landscape assets. In other words, the sector could be identified and estimated on the basis of the economic activities intended to satisfy demand for heritage assets, regardless of the characteristics of the products and production processes involved. In particular, drawing on the NACE Rev.2 classification of production sectors, the economic activities designed to meet the demand for cultural goods and landscapes could be considered those covered by sections C-G-I-J-M-N-O-P-R-S (Table 1.4).

Table 1.4 Economic activities intended to meet the demand for cultural heritage assets according to the NACE Rev.2 classification (ISTAT, 2009)

Section	Description
A	Agriculture, forestry and fishing
B	Mining and quarrying
C	Manufacturing
D	Electricity, gas, steam and air conditioning supply
E	Water supply; sewerage, waste management and remediation activities
F	Construction
G	Wholesale and retail trade, repair of motor vehicles and motorcycles
H	Transportation and storage
I	Accommodation and food service activities
J	Information and communication
K	Financial and insurance activities
L	Real estate activities
M	Professional, scientific and technical activities
N	Administrative and support service activities
O	Public administration and defence, compulsory social security
P	Education
Q	Human health and social work activities
R	Arts, entertainment and recreation
S	Other service activities
T	Activities of households as employers; undifferentiated goods- and services-producing activities of households for own use
U	Activities of extraterritorial organisations and bodies

In detail, the following activities are involved in meeting the demand for heritage assets:

- manufacturing (section C), such as the reproduction of recorded media (class 18.2) (e.g. museum audio-video guides);
- wholesale and retail trade (section G), such as retail sale of new goods in specialised stores (including art galleries) (class 47.78);
- accommodation and food service activities (section I), with reference to all classes;
- information and communication (section J), such as computer programming, consultancy and related activities (class 62.0) and data processing, hosting and related activities and web portals (class 63.1);
- professional, scientific and technical activities (section M), such as architectural activities (landscape architecture) (class 71.11);
- administrative and support service activities (section N), such as landscape service activities (class 81.3);
- public administration and defense (section O), such as the regulation of the activities of providing health care, education, cultural services and other social services (class 84.12);
- education (section P), such as cultural training (class 85.52);
- arts, entertainment and recreation (section R), such as the activities of libraries, archives, museums and other cultural activities (class 91.0);
- other service activities (section S), such as activities of other membership organisations (class 94.99) including those pursuing cultural aims.

This list is clearly illustrative and not exhaustive. The heterogeneity that characterises heritage assets, in fact, does not allow us to exclude the possibility, *ex ante*, that other production sectors are also involved in satisfying their demand. Therefore, the list should be adapted according to the cultural and landscape asset under analysis.

Macroeconomic performance indicators for heritage assets

After defining a possible strategy for identifying the heritage assets sector, we now move on to consider which performance indicators can best quantify their contribution to a country's economic development. There are many useful approaches to measuring the economic potential of cultural heritage and, with it, heritage assets. These include the approaches of Cultural Statistics, ESSnet-Culture, UNESCO, OECD, UNCTAD, the World Intellectual Property Organization (WIPO), KEA European Affairs and, within Italy, the Symbola Foundation and Unioncamere. Each of these approaches is based on certain macroeconomic key indicators (e.g. value added, employment, exports, etc.), which are grouped into macro-categories that measure, in most cases, the *direct* impact of the cultural heritage sector on the economy.

Table 1.5 Performance indicators of the heritage assets sector

Market structure
- Number of enterprises
- Volume of production
- Profits
- Added value
- Salaries

Employment
- Primary direct employment rate
- Secondary direct employment rate
- Indirect employment rate
- Induced employment rate

Foreign trade
- Value and volume of exports
- Value and volume of imports
- Trade balance (difference between the value of exports and imports)

Innovation
- Input (human, physical and financial capital initially employed)
- Processes (resources used in the next steps)
- Output (revenue, profits, return on innovation, patents, scientific publications)

Environmental sustainability
- Energy efficiency
- Load capacity

Starting from these approaches, in what follows we propose a list of indicators limited to only those that are more appropriate for the performance analysis of heritage assets rather than cultural heritage in the broader sense. These indicators can be traced back to five main categories (Table 1.5): (i) market structure and characteristics, (ii) employment, (iii) foreign trade, (iv) innovation and (v) environmental sustainability. The first three categories include indicators that are more oriented towards quantifying the economic performance of heritage assets, while the last two extend the assessment to more qualitative aspects; for this reason, they will be analysed separately in Chapter 2.

Market structure

Market structure indicators measure simply market characteristics in terms of the number of enterprises, production volume, revenues, added value (in terms of contribution to GDP) and salaries paid to employees.

Employment

The employment category includes indicators aimed at measuring employment rates within the heritage assets and related sectors. From a macroeconomic perspective, heritage assets can take on particular import-ance in terms of their ability to generate employment. It is well known that the quantity of labour necessary to obtain a certain level of production is inversely proportional to the marginal productivity of the work (i.e. the vari-ation in the quantity of work necessary to produce an additional unit of a good). The higher the productivity of the work, the smaller the amount of labour required, given a specific level of technology. Technological improvements thereby increase the marginal productivity of the work, redu-cing the amount of labour demanded. Consequently, in order to estimate the employment impact determined by the heritage assets sector, it is necessary to assess the productivity levels of the sector's different types of employment, distinguishing among direct (primary and secondary), indirect and induced employment.

Primary direct employment refers to the supply and demand of qualified and specialised services. In particular, it comprises a variety of professional skills (e.g. technical-scientific, managerial and administrative) that demon-strate little to no seasonality and substantial independence from activities carried out in other sectors. For some years, demand for primary employ-ment in the heritage assets sector has been undergoing profound change in terms of the professional profiles required. Alongside demand for traditional figures (e.g. archaeologists, architects, art historians, restorers, archivists, librarians, etc.), demand is also increasing for new professional profiles, such as bioarchaeologists, archaeologists, archaeozoologists, archaeobotanists, archaeometrists, geoarchaeologists, structural engineers, planners, geologists and museum professionals. These professionals are expected to contribute sig-nificantly to the protection and enhancement of heritage assets. Finally, the marked qualification and differentiation of professional figures in the primary labour market for this sector requires an equally qualified and differentiated employment offer.

Direct secondary employment, on the other hand, refers to general and low-skilled services. It is largely based on the interaction between an unskilled labour demand for time-limited periods and a supply that tends to be comprised of marginal components of the available labour force.

Indirect employment includes the total amount of labour employed to implement the production of intermediate goods and services in the heritage assets sector. As assets in this sector may be considered tourist attractions, labour employed indirectly may be affected by the seasonal nature of tourism.

Finally, induced employment comprises the total workforce employed in productive activities that have developed as a result of expenditure by the sector of cultural and landscape assets. Such employment is generally not affected by the employment and production characteristics of the heritage assets sector, being in no way integrated into the production processes that support it. Induced employment is particularly relevant, as it is a measure of the multiplier effects of the cultural and landscape assets sector.

Foreign trade

The third category includes indicators aimed at measuring the performance of heritage assets in relation to the international flow of cultural tourism, including the value and volume of exports, the value and volume of imports and the value difference between exports and imports (i.e. the 'trade balance'). The growing internationalisation of cultural tourism makes it extremely important to assess the effects of foreign exchange inflows on the economies of the receiving countries. Foreign demand for heritage assets not only changes the balance of international transactions but it can also create employment and income within the recipient countries. The effect of international cultural tourism on the balance of payments becomes, therefore, a relevant factor both for analysing the role of cultural tourism in making trade ties with foreign countries less stringent, and for assessing the capacity of an economic system to internalise the multiplier effects of foreign demand, as presented in the following section. In this regard, it should be noted that the accounting tools that are conventionally used to quantify both of the earlier-mentioned aspects are insufficient, as they only consider the direct effects of tourism activity and neglect the indirect and induced effects.

If we analyse the tourist balance – that is the difference between foreign tourist consumption in Italy and the foreign tourism of Italian residents – we can see that the foreign currency revenues that derive from foreign tourist demand do not include the value of indirectly stimulated imports. Another relevant aspect to consider is the extent to which the heritage assets sector is able to influence international economic relations. To this end, it is important to separate the consumption of cultural and landscape assets by the resident population from that of the foreign population. In other words, it is worth distinguishing between internal consumption (i.e. that of residents and non-residents for Italian heritage assets) and national consumption (i.e. that of residents for all heritage assets, both within and outside Italy). If, in fact, the focus of the analysis concerns the economic impact of heritage assets on the local economy, it is necessary to concentrate on internal consumption, since national consumption is of no use because it also includes a demand that will stimulate other national economies. In contrast, national consumption assumes particular importance when the analysis is directed to the economic effects of heritage assets on the balance of payments.

Innovation and environmental sustainability

Both the innovation and the environmental sustainability categories include qualitative indicators of the performance of heritage assets. Accordingly, and as previously mentioned, they will be analysed separately in Chapter 2.

Heritage assets and multiplier effects

While the indicators discussed in the previous section are useful for measuring the direct impact of the heritage assets sector on the economic system, they fail to capture its possible multiplier effects. Unlike goods that can be consumed in places other than their production origin, heritage assets – such as landscapes, cultural assets and tourist attractions – must be 'used' in the place where they are situated. This characteristic differentiates them substantially from other tourist goods and services – of which some can be consumed in other locations. If the geographical distribution of heritage assets coincides with the geographical distribution of productive activities, then the multiplier effects generated by increased demand for cultural tourism tend to remain geographically limited to the local context. If, in fact, consumption flows in the direction of a particular region where a cultural or landscape asset is located, the region may benefit from a multiplier effect on the local economy, in terms of both income and employment. The extent of this effect depends on two main factors: (i) the demand for heritage assets and (ii) the structural characteristics of the local production system.

In order to contribute significantly to the development of the local economy, demand for cultural tourism in a specific geographical area must be autonomous (i.e. not induced by other economic activities) and not occasional. Only if both of these conditions are met then heritage assets may generate multiplier effects and drive local development. These conditions are, in fact, sufficient to create production activity aimed at the direct satisfaction of tourist goods and services whose consumption is geographically confined, resulting in new employment opportunities and value added. This multiplier effect will be limited at the local level if some of the production activities are conducted outside the cultural or landscape asset area. In other words, to benefit most from multiplier effects, the local context must have production units available to offer the greatest number of goods and services induced by the demand for cultural tourism, at competitive prices. However, no local productive structure can competitively activate the production of all goods and services demanded for cultural tourism. Consequently, a more or less significant part of this production will necessarily be 'imported' from outside the area in which the heritage asset is located. Therefore, in the presence of an autonomous and not occasional demand for cultural tourism, in order for the local area to enjoy substantial multiplier effects, the efficiency and diversification of its productive structure must minimise the need for goods and services to be produced outside the local context.

Notes

1 Later, with Legislative Decree No. 86 of 12 July 2018, the delegation of tourism passed from the Ministry of Cultural Heritage and Activities to the Ministry of Agriculture.
2 Non-excludability can be of a technical nature (e.g. it is impossible to exclude someone from viewing a television broadcast) or an economic nature (e.g. it is impossible to exclude someone from using an asset due to excessive costs).
3 This is within certain limits, since, if the number of individuals exceeds a certain threshold, usefulness may decrease due to the resulting congestion (consider, e.g. a walk in the mountains).

4 While reporting mechanisms can reduce information asymmetries in the cultural tourism market, they can also increase the likelihood that heritage assets will be subject to towing and snobbish effects. Reviews of a cultural or landscape good, in fact, can increase demand for that good if the reviews are extremely positive or decreasing it in the opposite case (towing effect). Similarly, particularly positive reviews may reduce demand for a heritage asset by prompting some consumers to replace that asset with another with more exclusive characteristics (snobbish effect).

References

CISET (2018) "Il turismo culturale in Italia: Spesa, trend e comportamento dei visitatori". Report by M. Manente presented at the "TourismA – salone dell'archeologia e turismo culturale", Florence, 17 February 2018.

Cozzi, A.O. (2018) "Dimensione economica e dimensione culturale europea", Aedon, 2, ISSN 1127–1345.

D.L. n° 86, 12 luglio (2018) (Disposizioni urgenti in materia di riordino delle attribuzioni dei Ministeri dei beni e delle attività culturali e del turismo, delle politiche agricole alimentari e forestali e dell'ambiente e della tutela del territorio e del mare, nonché in materia di famiglia e disabilità) (18G00113). GU Serie Generale n. 160 del 12-07-2018.

D.lgs. n° 42, 22 gennaio (2004) (Codice dei beni culturali e del paesaggio). G.U. n. 45 del 24 febbraio 2004, s.o. n. 28.

Delbono, F. e Fiorentini, G. (1987) *"Economia del turismo"*. Studi Superiori NIS, La Nuova Italia Scientifica, Rome.

D'Auria, A. (2017) "Il valore dei beni culturali: paradigmi per un approccio non strumentale ad uno sviluppo heritage-based". In *"Sebastà Isolympia. Il patrimonio riscoperto, l'eredità culturale da valorizzare"*. Edited by Vito, G. Enzo Albano Edizioni, Naples (Italy), pp. 102–127.

Di Maio, A. e De Simone, E. (2006) "Alcune riflessioni economiche sulla fruizione dei beni culturali". *Web Journal on Cultural Patrimony*, 1, ISSN: 1827–8868.

Future Brand (2016) "Country Brand Index 2014–15" www.futurebrand.com/uploads/CBI2014-5.pdf.

ISTAT (2009) "Classificazione delle attività economiche Ateco 2007 derivata dalla Nace Rev. 2". Metodi e Norme n. 40.

L. n° 310 del 26 aprile (1964) (Costituzione di una Commissione d'indagine per la tutela e la valorizzazione del patrimonio storico, archeologico, artistico e del paesaggio). GU Serie Generale n.128 del 26-05-1964.

L. n° 71 del 24 giugno (2013) (Conversione in legge, con modificazioni, del decreto-legge 26 aprile 2013, n. 43, recante disposizioni urgenti per il rilancio dell'area industriale di Piombino, di contrasto ad emergenze ambientali, in favore delle zone terremotate del maggio 2012 e per accelerare la ricostruzione in Abruzzo e la realizzazione degli interventi per Expo 2015. Trasferimento di funzioni in materia di turismo e disposizioni sulla composizione del CIPE) (13G00117). GU Serie Generale n. 147 del 25-06-2013.

Lancaster, K.J. (1966) "A New Approach to Consumer Theory". *The Journal of Political Economy*, 74(2): 132–157.

UNESCO (2009) "The 2009 UNESCO framework for cultural statistics (FCS)". UNESCO Institute for Statistics, Montreal.

UNWTO (2005) "City tourism & culture. The European experience". Brussels, ETC Research Report No. 1.

UNWTO (2008) "International Recommendations for Tourism Statistics 2008". Studies in Methods Series M No. 83/Rev.1.

Volpe, G. (2018b) "Un patrimonio italiano". In "Italia rurale. Paesaggio, patrimonio culturale e turismo, Lezioni e pratiche della Summer School Emilio Sereni". Edited by Bonini, G. and Pazzagli, R., Edizioni Istituto Alcide Cervi, Gattatico, Reggio Emilia, Italy, pp. 71–88.

Volpe, G. (2018b) *"Un patrimonio italiano"*. Italia rurale: Paesaggio, patrimonio culturale e turismo. Quaderni 14. Edizioni Istituto Alcide Cervi.

2 Heritage assets, innovation and environmental sustainability

Introduction

In Chapter 1, we highlighted that, among the possible indicators of the performance of heritage assets, innovation and environmental sustainability represent two qualitative measures. Nonetheless, their importance was highlighted in the recent Strategic Plan for the Development of Tourism (2017), drawn up by the Permanent Committee for the Promotion of Tourism with the aim of providing Italy with a strategic direction in the field of tourism and culture. Outlining an 'organised system' of 4 general objectives, 13 specific objectives and 52 lines of action over the period 2017–2022, the plan defines 'innovation' and 'sustainability' as two of the three transversal principles (together with 'accessibility') to be considered when drawing up strategies, objectives and interventions. These must therefore contribute, on the one hand, to innovating the products, processes, technologies and organisation of cultural and non-cultural tourism and, on the other hand, to improving the sustainability of tourism in its various meanings relating to the environment, the local context, heritage conservation, socio-economics, culture and citizenship. Such cross-cutting tasks can be appropriately traced back to the themes of both innovation and sustainability.

The importance of innovation lies mainly in the opportunities it generates for heritage assets to expand their tourist use in light of technological and market transformations. It also entails the emergence of new skills and, consequently, related training needs, with extremely positive effects in terms of employment. The theme of sustainability, on the other hand, relates to the sustainable management and use of heritage assets, in recognition of the positive externalities they can generate.

Innovation in the heritage assets sector

Definition and measurement of innovation

According to the *Oslo Manual* – elaborated by the OECD and the European Commission (2005) – innovation represents: 'the implementation of a new or significantly improved product (good or service), or process, a new marketing method, or a new organisational method in business practices, workplace organisation or external relations'. This definition includes a wide range of possible innovations. More precisely, with respect to the object, innovation may be divided into four main categories: product, process, marketing and organisational innovation. 'Product innovation' refers to the introduction of a good or service that is either new or significantly improved in terms of its characteristics or the uses for which it is designed; this may include a substantial improvement in technical characteristics, components and materials, embedded software, ease of use or other functional characteristics. 'Process innovation' refers to the implementation of a new or significantly improved method of production or distribution; this may include a significant change in techniques, technology, equipment and/or software. 'Marketing innovation' refers to the implementation of a new marketing method that involves a significant change in the design, market positioning, promotion or price of a product. Finally, 'organisational innovation' refers to the implementation of a new organisational method in the workplace, in terms of internal organisation or external relations. It is worth noting that, according to the Oslo Manual, in order to be qualified as innovation, the resulting product, process, marketing characteristic or organisational method must be new or significantly improved. It must also have been implemented (i.e. introduced into the market and used). Due to this second aspect innovations can be distinguished from inventions, with the latter characterised by the fact that they have not yet been implemented.

It is also possible to classify innovations according to the novelty of the results in terms of incremental, radical and breakthrough innovations. 'Incremental innovation' involves the modification, refinement, simplification, consolidation and improvement of existing products, processes, services and production and distribution activities. 'Radical innovation' implies, instead, the introduction of new products or services that cause considerable changes and generate new values. Finally, 'breakthrough innovations' (or 'revolutionary innovations') focus on generating surprise. They are rare and derive from scientific or engineering intuitions; for this reason, they are considered revolutionary – innovations that realise what had previously been thought to be impossible.

In terms of their origin, innovation can be classified as 'top-down innovation' (TDI) and 'bottom-up innovation' (BUI). In the case of TDI, innovation takes place from top to bottom; accordingly, the definition of targets and objectives and allocation of economic resources is set at the top of the structure and implementation is led by lower-level staff. Such innovation, therefore, takes the structure of a directive. In contrast, BUI occurs from the bottom up and, accordingly, can be generated by anyone in an organisation. It provides space for ideas from all staff, and not only from management.

Finally, other classifications of innovations that are less relevant for an analysis of the heritage assets sector include those based on the source of the innovation (i.e. stemming from R&D activities) and those based on strategies (i.e. open, closed, sustainable or disruptive).

It is clear that the incidence of certain types of innovation is definitely limited within the heritage assets sector, in which innovation is essentially incremental rather than radical and where it is possible to identify organisational and marketing innovations, TDI and BUI and very few process innovations.

In this sector, innovation can be measured using a number of different parameters that classify (i) the degree of innovation and (ii) the benefits stemming from innovation. In order to carry out such an analysis, it is necessary to consider three elements: inputs, processes and outputs. Inputs represent the resources (human, physical and financial) that feed the processes that generate the final result (i.e. the output); they can be measured on the basis of the financial resources used, the staff employed, the number of ideas generated, the expected result etc. As regards processes, it is possible to quantify the resources employed – in each individual project and on average – and the quantity of ideas that move from one phase of the process to another. Finally, in the case of outputs, measurement can refer to the quantity of new products or services launched, incremental increases in revenue and profits, the return on investment (ROI) of innovative activities and indirect outputs that do not generate liquidity but are important to measure, such as the number of patents or scientific publications.

Technological innovation and digitalisation

One form of innovation that is particularly important for the heritage assets sector is technological innovation, which can provide significant opportunities to enhance the value of cultural and landscape assets by improving their usability and, in general, modernising their offer. Technological innovation is characterised by transversality with respect to most of the types of innovation discussed in the previous section: it can relate to products, processes and organisation and marketing strategies, and it can also form the basis for both incremental and radical innovations. Its importance in the heritage assets sector is demonstrated by a survey carried out in 2009 in Italy by the Tagliacarne Institute for Unioncamere, which found that more than 70% of companies operating in the cultural heritage sector attaches prime importance to technological development (Tagliacarne Institute, 2009). Although the majority of firms recognises the importance of innovation, the highest percentage (65.3%) is recorded in central Italy, followed by the north of the country (approximately 60%) and the south and islands (51.9%).

Technological innovation can be an important tool for extending the use of cultural and landscape assets that are currently not (or only scarcely) usable due to, for example technical or safety issues. In particular, technology can be an important means for developing competitive business models based on the dissemination of heritage assets knowledge while limiting the risks inherent in their conservation and maintenance (Lazzaro, 2017). Other areas in which technological innovation can have a significant impact include:

- the conservation of extremely fragile landscape assets that require continuous monitoring, conservation and security;
- the diffusion, through digital means, of the social and ethical value of a region's heritage assets, transforming them into recognised assets by the local population through a progressive and stable path of social inclusion over time;
- dematerialisation, in terms of the digitisation and transmission of data on poorly connected cultural and landscape assets, enabling the creation of databases that include strategic information for operators in the heritage assets and related sectors;
- internal and external communication, through the progressive transfer of skills and improvement of best practices in the heritage assets sector, which are often characterised by a poor predisposition to network action;
- technologies for 'digital natives', enabling experiential use of heritage assets via 3D technology, virtual reality and augmented reality systems.

A large proportion of technological innovation in the heritage assets sector is therefore represented by digitisation. First, new digital technologies for cataloguing, reproducing, retrieving and presenting works in a digital format improve the accessibility of cultural and landscape assets, enabling anyone – from across the globe and at any time – to access them. Such technologies can take the form of, for example museum websites and applications for smart devices (e.g. smartphones and tablets) that disseminate knowledge about cultural and landscape assets and provide new models for presenting the offer of heritage assets. In particular, globalisation via digitalisation can contribute to safeguarding a region's cultural identity, making it easier to recover and pass on to future generations the identity value of a cultural asset or landscape and to disseminate cultural knowledge (Lazarus, 2017).

In addition to contributing to the globalisation of cultural content, digitisation can also significantly improve the local usability of heritage assets. In fact, digital technologies (e.g. modern audio and video guides or applications for smart devices) can be used to support traditional tourism around a cultural asset or landscape by extending visitors' enjoyment and knowledge. They can also provide visitors with a 'virtual visit' of a heritage asset; rather than replacing a traditional visit, this virtual visit could simply enrich their tourist experience. Such virtualisation, moreover, is particularly useful for extending the tourist experience to people with disabilities, as well as for helping individuals decide whether or not to visit a particular cultural or landscape asset. From this perspective, as discussed in Chapter 1, technological innovation has contributed to significantly reduce information asymmetries relating to heritage assets, creating 'reporting' mechanisms that enable potential asset users to make more informed consumer/use decisions.

Digital technology also facilitates the customs clearance of the cultural content of heritage assets. Such clearance was once perceived as a tool for intellectual enrichment and the exclusive prerogative of a cultural elite or handful of amateurs or experts. Now, digital technology is able to broaden the market of potential users of cultural and landscape assets, making such assets accessible to most.

Other than assisting heritage asset users, digital technologies can be of help for heritage asset operators. For example the use of technology for the restoration or the digital reconstruction of art is particularly useful for the purposes of study and scientific research.

Finally, many organisational and marketing innovations in the heritage assets sector also founds on digitisation, in terms of the viral distribution of information, the expansion of knowledge tools and changes in consumer decision making processes, as previously discussed. Moreover, big data can considerably contribute to refining the techniques of predictive marketing in cultural tourism, facilitating a better understanding of market trends.

Heritage assets and sustainable development

The widespread concept of 'sustainable development' was defined more than 30 years ago by the President of the World Commission on Environment and Development Gro Harlem Brundtland, in a report entitled *Our Common Future*. According to Brundtland, development is sustainable if it guarantees 'the needs of current generations without compromising the ability of future generations to meet their own needs' (World Commission on Environment and Development, 1987). The central element of this definition is the need for intergenerational equity, whereby future generations enjoy the same rights as current generations. The success achieved by this – mainly ecological – definition has animated an international debate, leading to numerous in-depth studies of sustainability that, over time, have extended to all dimensions of development. In particular, the three primary dimensions considered are (i) environmental, (ii) economic and (iii) social. 'Environmental sustainability' refers to the ability to preserve, over time, the three functions of the environment: to supply resources, receive waste and serve as a direct source of utility (well-being). 'Economic sustainability', on the other hand, refers to an economy's ability to generate sustainable growth by effectively combining resources and enhancing the specificity of regional products and services. Finally, 'social sustainability' represents the ability to guarantee that conditions of human well-being (i.e. safety, health, education) are equally distributed across classes and genders. Sustainable development, therefore, represents the path to achieving a long-term balance between the three dimensions that characterise community development, supported by underlying policies.

In the framework of cultural and landscape assets, the topic of sustainability may not seem immediately evident. Agenda 2030 for Sustainable

Development – defined in 2015 by the governments of the 193 member countries of the UN – implies that heritage assets play an absolutely marginal role in achieving the 17 objectives, mentioning them only once, within objective 11 ('Make cities and human settlements inclusive, safe, resilient and sustainable'); this is then linked, in sub-objective 11.4, to efforts to strengthen protection for heritage assets ('Strengthen efforts to protect and safeguard the world's cultural and natural heritage') (UN, 2015). Greater recognition of the contribution of cultural and landscape heritage to sustainability can be found in the New Urban Agenda (the draft of which was adopted in 2016 by the UN at the 'Housing and Sustainable Urban Development – Habitat III' conference; the final version was published in the following year), in which heritage assets are mentioned several times (UN, 2017). Similarly, international organisations such as UNESCO and the International Council on Monuments and Sites (ICOMOS) have highlighted the importance of cultural and landscape heritage in sustainable development (Nocca, 2017). Some authors (see, e.g. Mergos, 2017) even consider the protection and enhancement of heritage assets a possible fourth dimension of sustainability along with environmental, economic and social dimensions.

In the following, the link between heritage assets and sustainable development is analysed with specific reference to the environmental dimension. The discussion is developed on two levels, first considering heritage assets as cultural and landscape assets and subsequently considering such assets as tourist attractions.

Environmental sustainability of heritage assets as cultural and landscape assets

When heritage assets are conceived as cultural and landscape assets, the issue of environmental sustainability is linked to the analysis of two main management aspects, namely energy saving and the use of renewable energy sources. Both of them are so strongly connected to the heritage sector (energy saving can *also* be achieved through the use of renewable energy sources) that, in 2015, MIBACT drafted comprehensive guidelines for improving energy efficiency in the heritage assets sector (including historical and urban centres and cores), in which it also outlined the opportunities, limitations and criticalities of renewable sources.

In recent years, energy saving has become increasingly important – so much so that it is among the main objectives of many national governments. First and foremost, the importance placed on energy saving stems from the need for public administrations to rationalise public spending and reduce the costs incurred in running buildings (in which the supply of energy and fuel is critical). Energy saving is also needed to significantly reduce the emissions of pollutants (e.g. carbon dioxide) into the atmosphere, thus determining important benefits for the environment. However, when applied to cultural and landscape assets, energy saving policies require very careful examination.

For example the case of historical buildings – heritage assets for which improvements to energy performance generally involve significant structural changes – require a specific in-depth evaluation (Box 2.1).

Box 2.1 *Energy savings in historical buildings resulting from the* Guidelines for the Improvement of Energy Efficiency in Cultural Heritage *(MIBACT, 2015)*

In historical buildings, the improvement of energy performance (i.e. the annual amount of energy consumed or expected to be consumed to meet the various needs associated with standard use of the building, including air conditioning, hot water production, ventilation and lighting) involves architectural changes. Such changes must be carefully designed on the basis of a precise energy diagnosis, in order to avoid the risk of jeopardising the monumental and/or documentary value of the building to the point of compromising its static safety. The energy diagnosis:

1. defines the energy balance of the building, identifying the possible recovery of dispersed energies;
2. assesses the necessary conditions of thermohygrometric well-being and safety and identifies appropriate energy saving solutions;
3. evaluates energy saving opportunities from a technical-economic perspective, optimising building management methods such as energy supply contracts.

These operations, however, can be particularly complex in historical buildings due to a lack of adequate plants and sections, in addition to a frequent lack of knowledge of the associated stratigraphy and the materials of the internal and external walls.

In general, measures to optimise the energy performance of historical buildings are based on three types of action:

1. thermal insulation of the building envelope;
2. implant interventions;
3. lighting interventions.

The first type of action optimises the amount of thermal energy that the building is able to exchange with the external environment. To this end, it is desirable, during winter months, both to encourage the production and accumulation of heat and to limit heat loss to the external environment. This can be achieved by exploiting solar energy and optimising the free thermal inputs generated inside the building as a byproduct of other processes (as in the case of heat produced by users and/or appliances and devices) and reducing the flow of heat between two environments at different temperatures (i.e. improving overall thermal insulation). The second and third types of action, on the other hand, aim at improving the performance of energy production systems inside the building (e.g. thermal and cooling energy systems) and lighting systems through, for example the installation of LED bulbs. The combined use of these actions makes it possible to reduce demand for energy while achieving optimal comfort conditions.

As regards renewable energy sources, the guidelines argue that management of heritage assets should be carried out in line with environmental sustainability objectives. This is because, unlike fossil fuels, renewable energy cannot be exhausted and therefore the share of resources for future generations remains unchanged. The most widespread renewable energy source for heritage assets is solar, whereas other renewable energy sources (e.g. heat pumps, biomass and geothermal energy) tend to play a negligible role. With respect to installation constraints of solar systems, Presidential Decree No. 31 of 13 February 2017 repealed the previous Presidential Decree No. 139 of 9 July 2010 according to which, in restricted areas, solar, thermal and photovoltaic panels of up to 25 m^2 could exploit simplified authorisations. In particular, no authorisation is necessary in case of panels that are installed on flat roofs and that therefore are not visible from public outdoor spaces or those that are integrated into the roofs, excluding buildings reported in Art. 136, paragraph 1, letters (b) and (c) of Legislative Decree No. 42 of 22 January 2004 (Code of Cultural Heritage and Landscape), i.e. villas, gardens, parks and historical centres which require prior landscape authorisation. The rules and directives established by these landscape plans have a significant impact on the use of renewable energy resources such as photovoltaics and wind power.

Again, the case of historical buildings conveys the main technical issues related to the use of renewable sources in meeting the energy needs of heritage assets (Box 2.2).

Box 2.2 *Active and passive solar systems in historical buildings resulting from the* **Guidelines for the Improvement of Energy Efficiency in Cultural Heritage** *(MIBACT, 2015)*

Active solar systems capture, store and use solar radiation to produce electrical or thermal energy through photovoltaic or thermal systems included in the building's structures. The application of photovoltaic panels on the roofs of historical buildings is hardly an optimal solution, since the energy advantage obtained is relatively limited, and significant alteration of the building image is required. For this reason, it is preferable to secure alternative solutions, such as relocation of the photovoltaic system in an external solar field.

The poor cost-benefit ratio of photovoltaic systems also characterises solar collectors that transform solar energy into thermal energy to be used for underfloor and domestic water heating. In this case, the need for collectors to be close to the storage tank and distribution system in order to reduce heat loss makes it less feasible to place the panels at some distance from the historical building. In this event, it is necessary for them to be installed on the roof of the historical building.

Passive solar systems, on the other hand, are closely integrated into buildings and designed to improve the thermohygrometric and psycho-perceptive comfort of users without the use of external energy sources.

In this perspective, the building is conceived as a passive system, with a targeted distribution of interior spaces and a careful choice of materials, including specific glass surfaces and masonry. Depending on their position, passive solar systems can be 'lean to' (i.e. aggregated or leaning against the building, representing an outdoor extension) or 'embedded' (i.e. constituting a 'completion'). The former are less wide-spread than the latter, which require alterations to the original building structure. Passive solar systems, on the other hand, can be classified as 'direct gain', 'indirect gain' or 'isolated', depending on their operation. In direct gain systems, energy is generated or captured directly within the environment for which it is intended. In indirect gain systems, energy is captured or generated in a space adjacent to the recipient room and transferred through convection. Finally, in isolated systems, energy is collected and stored in a space away from the recipient environment and channelling systems are used for transmission. The latter, in particular, enable the air conditioning or lighting of heritage assets in particularly disadvantaged positions (e.g. hypogea, caves, etc.).

Finally, an important aspect to be considered in the energy requalification interventions of cultural and landscape heritage assets concerns their economic analysis, based on (i) the evaluation of the primary energy savings achieved by the intervention relative to the existing situation, (ii) the carbon dioxide emissions avoided and (iii) the investment profitability. The primary energy savings represent the annual savings of fossil energy – expressed in kWh/year – that the proposed solution would achieve over the existing energy system. Avoided carbon dioxide emissions are the difference in emissions obtained as a result of the redevelopment. To this end, it is possible to use an indicator given by the ratio between the cumulative discounted avoided emissions and the discounted investments necessary for the implementation of an innovative project, so as to avoid being limited to the purely economic value of the project. Finally, the investment profitability can be measured using specific indicators such as the net present value (NPV) or the internal rate of return (IRR) of the investment.

Environmental sustainability of heritage assets as tourist attractions

The analyses discussed above can be significantly expanded when heritage assets are conceived as tourist attractions, since this entails the need to ensure the environmental sustainability of tourist flows and preserve them from visitor overcrowding. If, on the one hand, the tourist attractiveness of a heritage asset is able to produce regional wealth, it is also able to spoil the cultural and landscape asset in a short span of time. Accordingly, if tourism – including cultural tourism – is not properly planned, managed and monitored, it can cause irreparable environmental, social and economic damages. Cultural tourism can, in fact, generate employment opportunities and support local industry by virtue of its transversality, which can promote growth and economic development at regional level; but it can also contribute to the over-use of local resources, pollution and, subsequently, degradation. It is clear, therefore, that tourism and the conservation of cultural and landscape heritage cannot exist independent of one another and that the preservation and management of natural and cultural resources represent a fundamental challenge for policy makers. Therefore, with respect to heritage assets, there is a need to develop 'sustainable' tourist flows, first from an environmental point of view.

The aims and principles of sustainable tourism should build on those of sustainable development: to guarantee individuals' ability to draw on present resources in a manner compatible with the need to protect and safeguard the resources and heritage of mankind. The Council of Europe defines sustainable tourism as 'any form of tourist activity which respects and preserves in the long term natural, cultural and social resources and which contributes positively and fairly to the economic development and well-being of the individuals living and working in these areas' (Council of Europe, 1997). This can be translated into the integrated management of all resources to meet economic, aesthetic and social needs while preserving cultural integrity, ecosystems, biodiversity and basic living conditions (UNWTO, 2005). The importance of sustainable development has also been recognised by the UN, which declared 2017 the international year of sustainable tourism.[1]

While the concept of sustainability is defined in economic, social and environmental dimensions that correspond with the three objectives to be pursued simultaneously (i.e. sustainable economic growth, social progress and the protection and promotion of the environment), the concept of sustainable tourism founds on:

- the opportunity for local communities to benefit from tourism, in terms of higher income and quality of life;
- the opportunity for visitors to enjoy a quality tourist experience;
- the protection and safeguarding of environmental resources.

The Travel & Tourism Competitiveness Index (TTCI), adopted by the World Economic Forum, periodically analyses the competitiveness of the tourism sector in 136 countries around the world (i.e. those comprising 98% of global GDP). To this end, it considers 14 dimensions of tourism, organised in four areas of competitiveness (sub-indices):

- the 'enabling environment', which captures the business environment, safety and security, health and hygiene, human resources and the labour market and innovative and technological infrastructure;
- 'travel & tourism policy and enabling conditions', which captures the degree to which policies prioritise tourism, international openness, price competitiveness and environmental sustainability;
- 'infrastructure', which covers the infrastructure for air, land and sea transport as well as infrastructure serving the tourism sector, specifically;
- 'natural and cultural resources', which captures the amount and characteristics of the natural and cultural resources.

It is interesting to note that the latest available data (updated to 2017) place Italy in the 8th place internationally. Disaggregating the data, we may easily note the importance of heritage assets for the Italian tourism sector, as such assets enable the country to be ranked 5th internationally for cultural resources and 12th for natural resources. However, Italy ranks only 37th overall for environmental sustainability in the tourism sector. Further disaggregating the data, it is interesting to observe that Italy is ranked 1st for the number of cultural World Heritage Sites, 11th for the number of natural World Heritage sites and only 106th (out of 136) for the 'sustainability of travel and tourism industry development' (Table 2.1).

The picture that emerges confirms the results of the analysis carried out in Chapter 1 on the importance of heritage assets as a driving force for the tourism sector, highlighting that, in the case of Italy, the sector is still far behind in terms of the environmental sustainability of tourism flows.

Seasonality and the carrying capacity of heritage assets

One of the main threats to environmental sustainability is the seasonal nature of tourist flows, which can have a significant impact on cultural and landscape assets and subject them, for a short period of the year, to significant demographic pressure. With the aim of guaranteeing heritage asset with a sustainable tourist flow, it is necessary to differentiate tourist 'loads', thereby reducing seasonality. To this end, different strategies may be adopted based on the maturity of the tourist attraction and whether it is a prevailing or emerging (e.g. smaller city of art, village, protected area, park, etc.) cultural or landscape asset. In the case of prevailing assets, policies of price differentiation and incentives to favour certain categories of users (e.g. school groups, students, pensioners) may be employed to attract visitors in the low

Table 2.1 Tourism Competitiveness Index for Italy, 2017, disaggregated data

Sub-index: Natural and cultural resources				Sub-indexes: travel and tourism policy and enabling conditions	
Dimension	Position	Dimension	Position	Dimension	Position
CULTURAL RESOURCES AND BUSINESS TRAVEL	5°	NATURAL RESOURCES	12°	ENVIRONMENTAL SUSTAINABILITY	37°
Number of cultural World Heritage Sites	1°	Number of natural World Heritage Sites	11°	Stringency of environmental regulations	53°
Oral and intangible cultural heritage (number of expressions)	22°	Total known species	71°	Enforcement of environmental regulations	84°
Sports stadiums (number of large stadiums)	10°	Total protected areas (% of total region)	50°	Sustainability of travel and tourism industry development	106°
Number of international association meetings (3-year average)	6°	Natural tourism digital demand (0–100 (best))	6°	Particulate matter (2.5) concentration ($\mu g/m^3$)	108°
Cultural and entertainment tourism digital demand (0–100 (best))	7°	Attractiveness of natural assets	57°	Environmental treaty ratification (0–27 (best))	20°
				Baseline water stress (5–0 (best))	101°
				Threatened species (% total species)	80°
				Forest cover change (% change)	27°
				Wastewater treatment (%)	21°
				Costal shelf fishing pressure – (tonnes/km^2)	36°

Source: author's elaboration on data from the World Economic Forum.

season. In the case of emerging assets, however, it may be more desirable to strengthen the typification and uniqueness of the asset within the framework of a national strategy for tourist enhancement. In this way, heritage assets that are less known but demonstrate high tourist potential could benefit from a better distribution of tourist flows that, in connection with the most successful destinations, would contribute to expanding the national offer of cultural tourism.[2]

An analytical tool that can be used to measure the demographic pressure exerted on a heritage asset is the 'Tourism Carrying Capacity Assessment' (TCCA), which was developed in 1997 by UNEP through the Priority Action Programme. This is a particularly flexible tool, as it can be adapted to different tourist realities and therefore used to plan and manage tourist flows. The World Trade Organization defines the TCCA as the maximum number of people who can visit, in the same period, a tourist destination without compromising its physical, economic and socio-cultural environment, and without negatively affecting the visitor experience (UNWTO, 2000). The assessment process is based on a careful study of the environment and all possible development scenarios, considering three parameters – political-economic, socio-demographic and physical-environmental – that are closely linked to a given region and its political management. It is important to point out that, although the TCCA has been addressed by many authors in the literature, there is, at present, no model of calculation that is universally applied, but only a number of different methodologies that were developed mainly in the 1990s. These include the methodology proposed by Cifuentes (1992) and those suggested by Van Der Borg and Costa (1995), Mansfeld and Jonas (2006) and UNEP (1997). The first three are based on a quantitative approach, whereas the UNEP method draws predominantly on qualitative analysis. In particular, the method developed by Cifuentes (1992) quantifies the TCCA in very practical terms, calculating the acceptable number of tourists from the surface of the tourist destination, corrected by a series of coefficients of different nature. This method is particularly useful for assessing tourist flows directed towards landscape assets – mainly protected areas and parks. Van Der Borg and Costa (1995), on the other hand, focus on the profitability of tourist flows. They solve a bound optimisation problem, maximising the function of income derived from tourism in a given region subject to a number of environmental, social and infrastructural constraints. Although this methodology was originally developed for the analysis of TCCA in historical centres, it was subsequently used for other types of heritage assets, including national parks. Mansfeld and Jonas (2006) proposed a method focused on the social aspects of TCCA, investigating the satisfaction of local residents. Finally, the qualitative method proposed by UNEP compares the status quo of cultural and landscape assets to different development scenarios, with the aim of defining guidelines for the future management of tourist flows. More recently, Cimnaghi et al. (2017) expanded the method proposed by Cifuentes (1992) in order to adapt it to the specific case of cultural heritage. In particular, the authors considered further variables such as accessibility (often difficult to guarantee completely, especially in the case of historical buildings), the ability to communicate the intrinsic value of cultural goods and the presence of any limitations (structural or security-related) due to legislative restrictions, while also bearing in mind the balance between the need for conservation and that for the enhancement of heritage assets. More precisely, they focused on different components of the TCCA, such as management value, theoretical value, physical/functional value, social value, psychological value and infrastructural/territorial value. Management TCCA was configured as a response to the weaknesses of the system by providing information on how to improve the tourism flows management in the local area. Theoretical TCCA was given by the maximum number of tourists who could find a place near the heritage asset; the relevant area was derived from the surface of the cultural asset location, with an area of 1 m^2 assigned to each tourist. Physical/functional TCCA was obtained from the theoretical TCCA, to which qualitative or quantitative corrective measures were applied, as derived from physical characteristics (e.g. elements that limited or prevented accessibility) or functional characteristics (e.g. safety conditions, architectural barriers) of the heritage asset. Social TCCA was obtained from an analysis of residents' perception of the tourist phenomenon, in both qualitative terms (e.g. seasonality of tourist flows, tourists' attitudes) and quantitative terms (e.g. number of visitors). Psychological TCCA was linked both to tourists' perception of the heritage asset and their level of satisfaction at the end of their visit (with respect to services, efficiency, etc.). Finally, infrastructural/territorial TCCA considered aspects related to infrastructural conditions (e.g. number of available car parks) and the adequacy of mobility policies (e.g. the capacity to receive, absorb and manage tourism flows) of the entire region in which the heritage asset is located.

Notes

1 In order to orient strategies and actions concerning the protection and management of heritage assets, it is important to distinguish the concept of 'sustainable tourism' from that of 'responsible tourism'. The first refers to the tourist offer and, therefore, to the set of policies and strategies for the sustainable management of tourist attractions. The second refers to the demand for tourism and therefore concerns the adoption by tourists of travel behaviour that respects resources, places and people and that contributes to promoting the well-being of the local community.
2 In this context, the establishment of the 'Italian capital of culture' – conferred to numerous small and medium-sized cities, has enhanced cultural tourism, redeveloped regional areas, mitigated the impact of tourist pressure and, at the same time, expanded the offer of cultural tourism to lesser known and smaller Italian places, relative to large cities of art.

References

Cifuentes, M. (1992) "Determinacion de capacidad de carga turistica en areas protegidas". WWF-CATIE Costarica.

Cimnaghi, E., Mondini, G., and Valle, M. (2017) "La Capacità di Carico Turistica – Uno strumento per la gestione del patrimonio culturale". Quaderni della valorizzazione – NS 5, Direzione Generale Musei Servizio II - Gestione e valorizzazione dei musei e dei luoghi della cultura, Rome (Italy).

Consiglio d'Europa (1997) "Developpement Touristique Durable" n° 84.

D.lgs. n° 42 (22 gennaio 2004) "Codice di tutela dei beni culturali e paesaggistici".

D.lgs. n° 42 (22 gennaio 2004) "Codice dei beni culturali e del paesaggio". G.U. n. 45 del 24 febbraio 2004, s.o. n. 28.

DPR n° 139 (9 luglio 2010) "Regolamento recante procedimento semplificato di autorizzazione paesaggistica per gli interventi di lieve entità". G.U. n. 199 del 26 agosto 2010.

DPR n° 31 (13 febbraio 2017) "Regolamento recante individuazione degli interventi esclusi dall'autorizzazione paesaggistica o sottoposti a procedura autorizzatoria semplificata". G.U. n. 68 del 22 marzo 2017.

Economic World Forum (2017) "The Travel & Tourism Competitiveness Report 2017 – Paving the way for a more sustainable and inclusive future". Downloadable from: www3.weforum.org/docs/WEF_TTCR_2017_web_0401.pdf.

Istituto Tagliacarne (2009) "Il sistema economico integrato dei beni culturali". Uniocamere – MIBACT.

Lazzaro, A. (2017) "Innovazione tecnologica e patrimonio culturale tra diffusione della cultura e regolamentazione". Federalismi.it.

Mansfeld, Y., and Jonas, A. (2006) "Evaluating the socio-cultural carrying capacity of rural tourism communities: A 'value stretch' approach". *Tijdschrift voor Economische en Siciale Geografie*, 97(5): pp. 581–599.

Mergos, G. (2017) "Cultural heritage and the economic development agenda". In Eds Mergos, G. and Patsavos, F., *Cultural Heritage and Sustainable Development: Economic Benefits, Social Opportunities and Policy Challenges*. Crete: Technical University of Crete.

MIBACT (2015) "Linee di indirizzo per il miglioramento dell'efficienza energetica nel patrimonio culturale". Downloadable from: www.beniculturali.it/mibac/export/MiBAC/sito-MiBAC/Contenuti/MibacUnif/Comunicati/visualizza_asset.html_156066123.html.

Nocca, F. (2017) "The role of cultural heritage in sustainable development: multidimensional indicators as decision-making tool". *Sustainability*, 9: 1882.

Oslo Manual (2005) *Guidelines for Collecting and Interpreting Innovation Data*. 3rd Edition. Paris: OECD.

Piano Strategico di Sviluppo del Turismo (2017) *PST 2017–2022. Italia Paese per Viaggiatori*. Rome: MIBACT.

UN (2015) "Transforming our world: The 2030 agenda for sustainable development". A/RES/70/1 Downloadable from: https://sustainabledevelopment.un.org/.

UN (2017) *New Urban Agenda*. New York: United Nations Habitat III Secretariat. ISBN: 978-92-1-132731-1.

UNEP (United Nation Environmental Program) (1997) "Guide to Good Practice in Tourism Carrying Capacity Assessment". Priority Actions Programme Mediterranean Action Plan.

UNWTO (United Nations World Tourism Organization) (2000) "Sustainable develop-
ment of tourism: A compilation of good practices". UNWTO Publications.
UNWTO (2005) "Making Tourism More Sustainable – A Guide for Policy Makers".
pp. 11–12.
Van der Borg, J., e Gotti, G. (1995) "The impact of tourism and visitor's Flow
Management". UNESCO/Venice-CISET.
World Commission on Environment and Development (1987) *Our Common Future*.
New York: Oxford University Press.

3 Financing heritage assets and art wealth management

Introduction

The aim of the present chapter is to determine which aspects are deemed particularly relevant for art sector financing, with respect to heritage assets and wealth management.

In particular, with regard to the theme of heritage asset financing, the chapter first explores the technique of project financing, which is considered particularly useful and suitable for financing the operations of cultural and environmental assets, on account of the average high requirement for funds, the complexity of operations and the often-mixed nature of public and private stakeholders. Following this, the chapter examines the theme of strategic, economic and financial planning through an analysis of the management instrument of the business plan, which is considered a necessary document in the public or private funding of heritage assets.

After analysing the main public funding opportunities of heritage assets in Italy and Europe and raising some critical reflections with regard to European and Italian gaps in the strategic coordination and planning of investment policies in the sector of cultural and landscape assets, the chapter ends with an overview of key themes in the management of invested assets in art and the development of services related to the art world.

Project financing as a useful instrument in the financing of heritage assets

When raising funds for the protection, conservation and enhancement of a heritage asset, the instrument of project financing is particularly useful, on account of the average high requirement for funds, the complexity of the operation and the often-mixed nature of public and private stakeholders.[1]

Project financing is a structured finance operation that is often used to finance long-term infrastructural projects. In the process, an investor considers, from the earliest stages, the financed project's cash flows and earnings, which will serve as the source of funds that will reimburse his or her financing (i.e. the project collateral), over and above the activities of the economic unit.[2]

Project financing lends itself to the funding of public works, which are often heritage assets. On the one hand, the financial technique enables public works to be maintained without public investment and, on the other hand, it is substantiated by funding a particular economic activity with a guaranteed flow of revenues to repay the investment.

In any project financial operation, the following stakeholders are generally involved:

- promoters (or driving entities), who generate project ideas and drive the project forward;
- a developer subject, who is chosen from among the promoters or recruited externally (if competences foreign to the promoters are required); this person takes care of the first-level analysis measuring the feasibility of the project, prepares the necessary strategic and operational plan and draws up prospective economic and financial plans;
- a lender subject, or the person (or persons) who finances the project;
- a financial advisor, who (in partnership with the developer) prepares economic and financial plans, manages relations with financial stakeholders and drafts financial reports; and
- a concession or project company (special purpose vehicle), which carries out the project and implements the legal and financial separation of the project from its investors.

In project financing, therefore, the economic analysis is generally carried out by the promoters, with the help of various professional figures. Furthermore, the establishment of a project company ensures that the project investment remains legally separate from the promoters' private assets. The promoters must therefore assess the project's ability to self-finance (i.e. the project's ability to generate sufficient cash flows to cover the investment and operating costs, to repay the cost of debt and to remunerate the invested capital, without further investment). As the assets of individual promoters remain legally distinct from the project, the various stakeholders are able to collaborate in support of the same business purpose. In the same way, the public and private subjects – comprising a heterogeneous group with a shared interest in and complementary contributions to the project – share the same risk because it is limited to the project itself and clearly divided between the parties. As highlighted above, this makes the technique particularly suitable for financing heritage assets, which are often public property but with private or mixed management. Through the technical tool of project financing, it is therefore possible to finance and enhance a public asset of cultural or environmental relevance, as it may gain profitability by, for example the concession in use for a specific time horizon to a special purpose vehicle that will take care of the protection, the conservation, the management and hopefully the economic and social valorisation, will pay a conventionally established annual fee or will correspond to the owner body a part of the revenue generated by the management, will reimburse the requested financing, will reap the right remuneration for the risk assumed and the capital employed and will return it to the agreed deadline to the public owner, and therefore to the community of that territory, enhanced and ready for a subsequent valorisation project.

Importance of the business plan and financial planning in the financing of heritage assets

As highlighted in the previous section, strategic, economic and financial planning are critical to the success of any heritage asset investment project; unfortunately, such planning tends to be significantly weak in Italy, in both the public and private sectors. The business plan is an operational tool that, when well-structured and drafted, represents a synthesis of the strategic, economic and financial planning processes. It is therefore an essential tool in the public and private financing of heritage assets.[3]

The business plan outlines the scope and characteristics of an entrepreneurial project, and it is used to plan, analyse, report on, and control the work. Its qualitative or descriptive part illustrates all the fundamental aspects of the entrepreneurial project, while its financial section outlines the expected results of the initiative in the form of a profit and loss statement, a balance sheet and a financial forecast. The business plan is therefore a hybrid qualitative and quantitative document that aims at analysing, planning and controlling a business strategy over a multi-year time horizon. In order to be useful for both the entrepreneur and the investor or project evaluator, the business plan must be clear, complete, reliable and transparent.[4]

Since each business plan must be drafted according to the peculiarities of the specific project, there is no standard template for its design. However, by way of example, the following are essential points that a complete business plan aimed at financing the protection, conservation or enhancement of a heritage asset should include:

1. presentation of the promoters and the company managing the asset;
2. description of the project and the business idea;
3. description of the product or service offered;
4. description of the reference market and demand;
5. definition of the commercial strategies;
6. description of the productive factors and technical-organisational feasibility;
7. an investment plan and analysis of the financial resources to be invested in the project; and
8. financial planning, including an income statement, balance sheet and financial forecast.

To prepare a complete and transparent business plan, it is first necessary to provide detailed information on the promoters and the company that will manage (or that currently manages) the heritage asset, describing the corporate structure, the mission (and possibly the company history), the business activities (either current or intended), the business model, the professional skills of the directors, the responsibility functions held, the governance and control model, the capital invested and any shareholdings in other companies held by the promoters.

It is also necessary to draft an executive summary of the entrepreneurial project, which should describe the product or service that is intended for the market, the reference market, the strategy, the organisational structure and the necessary resources. All of these elements are outlined in greater detail in the main body of the business plan, but they are first anticipated in the executive summary to give readers a first impression of the validity, consistency and profitability of the business idea – ideally an impression that invites them to continue reading.

Third, the plan must provide an in-depth description of the proposed product or service related to the heritage asset, highlighting the market need or demand that this product or service aims at satisfying, the life cycle of the product or service, the production methods and delivery, the time and costs required, the sale price, any collateral services offered, any alternatives available on the market and any relevant patents or licenses.

Fourth, the business plan must describe the characteristics of the reference market, providing a full analysis of the target customers and potential competitors. This analysis is necessary to form the assumptions for the projected income flows and business risks, which are presented later in the business plan, in the financial forecasts. In particular, it is necessary for the plan to define the composition and size of the demand presented by the reference market and the competitive positioning of the heritage asset and heritage management, compared to competing assets; this section should also highlight the market concentration, the existence and importance of any legislative barriers to managing or using the asset, the degree of differentiation of the bid and the competitive strategies of market leading and direct competitors, according to geographical location.

Fifth, in addition to outlining these details on the reference market, the business plan must also describe the intended commercial strategies in the form of a marketing plan. The marketing plan should draw on an in-depth SWOT analysis, in which strengths, weaknesses, opportunities and threats related to the project (from the perspective of the enterprise managing the asset) are presented and discussed.

Sixth, the business plan must analyse the general organisation of the productive factors (in particular, employees) and explore the feasibility of the initiative from a technical-organisational perspective.

Seventh, the plan should outline the necessary financial and human resources needed to drive the project over a multi-annual time horizon of reference.

Once the abovementioned qualitative and quantitative aspects are described, the business plan should end with financial planning in the form of a profit and loss statement, a balance sheet and a financial forecast; these items should extend the hypothesis and assumptions described in the previous sections of plan.

Having evaluated the feasibility of the overall business plan and determined – through the balance sheet and income statement – the patrimonial aggregates and final and prospective economic margins, the potential investor will be called to judge the sustainability and profitability of the proposed initiative by constructing balance sheet indexes and analysing the prospective financial statement.

A balance sheet index is the ratio between two or more values and aggregates of the balance sheet and income statement, appropriately reclassified according to the analyst's information needs. Capital ratios facilitate the analysis of a company's asset structure in order to ascertain conditions of equilibrium in the company's composition of loans and funding sources, as well as the correlations between classes. The first level of the analysis of capital strength is represented by individual indicators of loans and funding sources.

The indexes of composition are:

- the medium – to long-term indebtedness ratio, which is obtained from the ratio of consolidated liabilities to total assets (i.e. the balance sheet liability total) and expresses the degree of rigidity in the financial structure;
- the short-term debt index, which is obtained from the ratio of short-term liabilities to total assets or liabilities in the balance sheet, and expresses the degree of elasticity in the financial structure;
- the index of financial autonomy, which is obtained from the ratio between shareholder equity and total assets and expresses the company's level of capitalisation (i.e. degree of financial independence); and
- the total debt ratio, which is obtained from the ratio between third-party assets (i.e. liabilities) and total assets, and expresses the extent to which third-party capital contributes to covering the company's financial needs.

The loan composition indices are:

- the rigidity index of loans, which is obtained from the ratio between fixed assets and total assets in the balance sheet, and expresses the degree of rigidity in the company structure; and
- the index of elasticity of commitments, which is obtained from the ratio between current assets (i.e. short-term investments) and total assets, and expresses the degree of elasticity in the company structure.

The second level of analysis of capital strength concerns solidity indices, which consist of:

- the leverage ratio, which is obtained from the relationship between third-party assets (i.e. debts) and own resources, and expresses the extent to which equity capital contributes to covering the company's financial needs;
- the primary structure ratio, which is obtained from the ratio between shareholder equity and fixed assets and expresses the capacity of own resources to cover investments in fixed assets; and
- the secondary structure ratio, which is obtained from the ratio between the sum of net assets and consolidated liabilities and fixed assets, and expresses the extent to which assets are financed by durable sources.

Profitability indices are used to analyse the company's profitability by identifying the entity and origin of the company's income. The first level of the profitability analysis refers to the reclassified income statement, while the second level concerns profitability ratios such as:

- return on equity (ROE), which is obtained from the ratio between net profit and shareholder equity, and expresses the net return on equity (indicating the convenience of investing in the company as a shareholder);
- return on investment (ROI), which is obtained from the ratio between operating income and total assets, and expresses the return on total capital invested in the company, regardless of extra-characteristic events, financial events and the company's tax burden;[5]
- return on sales (ROS), which is obtained from the ratio between the operating result and turnover, and expresses the profitability of sales;
- turnover of invested capital, which is obtained from the ratio between turnover and total assets, and expresses the number of times in the year in which the total capital investment is renewed, through the turnover; and
- return on debts (ROD), which is obtained from the ratio between financial charges and financial payables, and expresses the average cost of funding sources.

Financial indicators are used to estimate the company's ability to face its financial needs without compromising the economic balance of its operations. This information is of a static nature, and it must therefore by complemented by an analysis of income flows, in order to generate a satisfactory judgment of the company's financial dynamics. At the first level of financial analysis, the financial management hedge ratio, obtained from the ratio between financial charges and operating income, provides information on the ability of the company's operating profitability to cover the cost of its debt (guaranteeing economic equilibrium). The lower the value of this ratio, the greater the company's capacity for repayment.

At the second level of financial analysis, the main liquidity indices used are the current ratio and the quick ratio. The former, which is obtained from the ratio between current assets and short-term liabilities, expresses the company's ability to meet short-term payables through liquid assets and financial resources released by short-term loans. The latter, which is obtained from the ratio between the sum of immediate and deferred liquid assets and short-term liabilities, expresses the company's ability to cope with short-term payables by using readily available monetary means.

In order for the index analysis to provide useful information, it must be compared to other index measures over time and space. In other words, it is necessary to compare the values of the indices of several financial years through a multi-year survey, as well as to draw appropriate comparisons with average values obtained by companies operating in the same sector through a spatial investigation.

In order to move from a static picture of a company's health to a dynamic one, index analysis must be combined with an analysis of financial flows. In fact, the analysis of financial flows includes a dynamic perspective that reveals the entity, origin and destination of resources handled over a certain period of time, tracing them back to specific areas of company management. The models used for the analysis of liquidity can be prepared *ex post* (i.e. at the time of management control), and therefore drawn up in the form of financial statements or a cash flow statement. They can also be formulated *ex ante* (i.e. at the time of planning). The purpose of financial statements is to provide useful financial information to the entrepreneur or investor to support their assessment of the company's financial balance (i.e. its solvency in the short and medium to long term) – in particular, the company's ability to cope in a timely and economic manner with the financial commitments connected with its management activity.

Public funding of heritage assets and European and Italian gaps in strategic coordination and planning

At both the European and national (i.e. Italian) levels, recent years have witnessed an increase in the number of public programmes designed to finance the protection, safeguarding and enhancement of artistic and cultural heritage assets.

In order to pursue the objectives of the European Agenda for Culture, the European Commission has financed several programmes for the period 2014–2020 under the Europe 2020 growth strategy. With these public funding programmes, the European Commission has showed a certain sensitivity to the immense cultural heritage that characterises the old continent as well as an awareness that this heritage, if adequately valued, could drive sustainable and lasting economic growth. The overall strategy and articulation of these European programmes (as presented in the Commission's external communication) aims at remedying a longstanding European gap in long-term strategic planning that previously led to high fragmentation and a lack of transnational and cross-sectoral connection and coordination.

However, despite these programmes, Europe has continued to demonstrate a lack of systematic effectiveness in its efforts to develop its artistic, environmental and cultural heritage into a strategic asset that will impart a competitive advantage to Europe over other global regions. As we shall see later, in Europe, significant differences exist between nations' strategies and models for enhancing artistic and cultural heritage, on account of the autonomy of European Union (EU) Member States and their different sensibilities.

The main public programmes for the protection of cultural heritage in Europe include:

- Creative Europe;
- Cultural Heritage and Global Change (JPICH);
- Horizon 2020 (III Pillar); and
- Interreg Europe (2014–2020).

Creative Europe is a framework programme providing 1.46 billion euros to the cultural and creative sector for the period 2014–2020. It is comprised of two sub-programs (Culture and MEDIA) and a cross-sector fund (i.e. a guarantee fund for the cultural sector and creative work, data support and piloting). Creative Europe pursues two general and four specific objectives.

The general objectives are to:

- promote and safeguard European linguistic and cultural diversity; and
- strengthen the competitiveness of the cultural and creative sector to promote intelligent, sustainable and inclusive economic growth.

The specific objectives are to:

- support the ability of the European cultural and creative sector to operate transnationally;
- promote the transnational circulation of cultural and creative works and cultural operators;
- reinforce the financial capacity of the cultural and creative sectors, especially small and medium-sized enterprises; and
- support transnational political cooperation to promote innovation, develop policy, build audiences and improve business models.

In more detail, Creative Europe supports:

- projects involving transnational cooperation between cultural and creative organisations, both inside and outside Europe;
- networks that help the cultural and creative sectors operate transnationally and strengthen their competitiveness;
- the translation and promotion of literary works through EU markets;

- platforms of cultural operators that promote emerging artists and stimulate an essentially European programming of cultural and artistic works;
- skills development and professional training for professionals in the audio-visual sector;
- the development of works of fiction, animation, creative documentaries and video games for the cinema and television markets and other platforms, both inside and outside Europe;
- film festivals promoting European films;
- funds for the co-production of international films;
- audience development in support of film literacy and interest in European films through a wide variety of events;
- European capitals of culture and the European heritage brand; and
- European awards for literature, architecture, heritage protection, cinema, and rock and pop music.

The joint initiative Cultural Heritage and Global Change (JPICH) was launched in December 2010 by the Council of the European Union in order to:

- investigate the relationship between tangible cultural heritage (e.g. historical cities, archaeological sites, museum collections, archives and libraries) and climate change, which is one of the most important factors of change for communities;
- deepen issues related to the protection and security of cultural heritage; and
- study the relationship between the protection of cultural heritage and its use by society.

The programme is based on the belief that cultural heritage and the management of cultural and landscape assets are contingent on environmental contexts, socio-economic frameworks and political and cultural attitudes, which are undergoing rapid and profound changes at the European level. It requires and justifies deep analysis and research activity to explore and predict current dynamics and future trends, in order to put appropriate and effective management into place and to guide assets in a profitable and sustainable direction. To this end, it seems entirely appropriate that this European programme finances highly innovative and interdisciplinary research projects aimed at:

- developing tools and models to understand the mechanisms of damage and degradation (including the effects of weathering and climate change) of tangible cultural heritage assets (including buildings, sites and landscapes);
- enhancing heritage assets through territorial planning to support quality of life and well-being in new and changing urban environments; and
- developing methods and tools for safeguarding the sustainable use of landscape elements and the re-use of sites and buildings.

In Italy, the deadline for funding applications to this program was 30 November 2017. Applications were invited from the private sector, universities and research institutes, and the total available funds amounted to 4.6 million euros.

Along the same lines, the specific objectives of challenge six of the Horizon 2020 programme are to support a greater understanding of Europe; promote solutions; and support inclusive, innovative and reflective societies. The programme was launched in the context of unprecedented transformations and growing global interdependencies, as well as the awareness that European cultural heritage could become an instrument of social integration and growth of extreme strategic importance. Challenge six builds on the legacy of the socio-economic and humanistic research (SSH) conducted by the Seventh Framework Program, giving more space to humanistic research and incorporating within it elements of information and communications technology, such as e-government. Research in the field of SSH is not limited to challenge six of Horizon 2020 but extends to all pillars of the Seventh Framework Program. Therefore, it is possible to carry out socio-economic and humanistic research, with particular attention to cultural heritage, in the context of projects funded by other areas of the Horizon 2020 programme. To date, the programme has allocated 1.158 million euros to the social challenge 'Europe in a changing world: Inclusive, innovative and reflective societies'.

Cultural heritage is among the several priorities of the Interreg Europe program (2014–2020), which, with specific reference to natural and cultural resources, aims at improving integrated environmental management for the protection and sustainable use of heritage and natural resources as well as improving the environmental management of urban areas to improve their quality of life. The programme funds projects seeking to develop and implement strategies to enhance and promote cultural and creative industries, also with the aim of supporting economic development and employment. The total allocation of funds (ERDF resources) for the programme over the period is approximately 359 million euros.

As described above, these public programmes aim at remedy a longstanding European shortcoming in long-term strategic planning, which, in recent years, has led to heavy fragmentation and a lack of top-level transnational and cross-sectoral connection and coordination. Although the cultural heritage sector is undoubtedly strategic at the European level (involving the direct and indirect employment of approximately 7.8 million persons), a unified and coordinated European strategy to enhance the region's immense cultural, artistic and environmental heritage is lacking. This lack of a true European industrial policy oriented towards cultural heritage as a tourist and economic resource is a missed opportunity, largely attributable to the structural defects of the EU, whereby the absence of political union has blocked the development of a structured and integrated European industrial policy. In this sense, the valorisation of artistic, environmental and cultural heritage assets has been negatively impacted, because culture is not among the exclusive competences of the EU or even among its competitive competencies (Arts. 3, 4 of the Treaty on the Functioning of the European Union); instead, it falls under Article 6 (i.e. an area in which the EU can only support, coordinate or complete the actions of Member States). Accordingly, the cultural heritage sector cannot be issued directives or European regulations, but only acts of soft law. Thus, aside from the abovementioned European funding opportunities and programmes dedicated to culture, the protection of cultural assets has always remained the responsibility of Member States; again, this has produced heavy fragmentation and a lack of unity across the adopted policies.

Moving to the national level, in recent years, the Italian government has issued various measures to finance projects aimed at protecting, safeguarding and enhancing the nation's artistic and cultural heritage. Among others, such measures include:

- the 'Culture and Development' National Operational Program (PON);
- the Art Bonus;
- museums and the development of territorial systems (i.e. MuSST); and
- dynamic museums.

In 2014, Italy presented to the European Commission the National Operational Program (PON) for 'Culture and Development', under the objective of 'Investment for growth and employment' in less developed regions of Italy. Following negotiations with the European Commission, the EU Decision of 12 February 2015 approved the 'Culture and Development' PON, co-funded by the European Regional Development Fund (ERDF 2014–2020) and national funds, to a total amount of approximately 491 million euros (of which 368.2 million euros was funded by the ERDF and 122.7 million by national co-financing).

The Ministry of Cultural Heritage and Activities and Tourism (MiBACT), administrator of the PON, delegates authority to regional governing bodies (MiBACT Regional Directorates, Superintendents) as part of a strategy to link the administrations of the five regions (Basilicata, Calabria, Campania, Puglia, Sicilia) with which specific Implementation Agreements (AOA) have been signed. The PON, in line with the policies outlined in the Europe 2020 Strategy, which define issues relating to the role of culture in the construction of an 'intelligent, sustainable, inclusive' society, aims at overcoming the under-utilisation of regional cultural resources in less developed regions of Italy by increasing their attractiveness, effecting more consistent flows of tourists, enhancing the cultural enjoyment and establishing (entrepreneurial and third sector) activities to support creative and cultural enterprises.

The PON strategy is articulated in three pillars, according to the relative programme axes:

- the first pillar aims at strengthening the demand and supply of cultural attractions under national ownership and/or demonstrating strategic relevance in Basilicata, Calabria, Campania, Puglia and Sicilia, also in terms of consolidating and qualifying services strictly connected to their cultural or touristic aspects;

- the second pillar aims at encouraging the growth of economic activities related to culture, with the intention of constructing and testing a policy to support competitiveness in the sector; it largely concerns economic profiles and social enterprises that contribute to increasing the attractiveness of the reference areas;
- the third pillar supports the overall management of the PON by improving the operational capabilities of the parties involved, pursuing efficiency objectives in the various areas concerned (administrative-procedural, organisational, technical) and encouraging implementation of the administrative strengthening plan.

The Art Bonus is a tax incentive that was introduced in 2014 to provide urgent provisions for the protection of cultural heritage assets, the development of culture and the revival of tourism. It provides a 65% tax relief for those who support public cultural heritage assets through financial donations. However, eligible cash disbursements must concern the maintenance, protection and restoration of public cultural assets; the support of institutions and places of culture and public belonging, such as museums, lyric-symphonic foundations and traditional theatres; the construction of new structures or the restoration of existing ones; or the support of public and non-profit bodies or institutions. The tax credit is divided into three equal annual instalments. In more detail, people or entities that do not carry out a commercial activity, such as employees or pensioners, can receive a maximum tax credit of 15% of their annual income, while those who carry out a commercial activity can receive a maximum 5% per thousand annual revenue.

Since its introduction in 2014 until the beginning of 2018, more than 1,000 entities have benefited from this measure: there have been approximately 1,300 domestic interventions and more than 200 million euros collected from approximately 6,000 patrons. The MiBACT data draw a profound imbalance in sums donated between the north and south of Italy, reflective of the deep disparities in industrial development and therefore economic conditions throughout the country. Interventions are, in fact, more concentrated in northern Italy, with Lombardy demonstrating the highest value of donations (78 million), followed by Veneto (over 30 million) and Piedmont (approximately 28 million). In stark contrast, there were no donations collected in Basilicata, 600 euros collected in Molise and 500 collected in Valle d'Aosta.

The 'Museums and Development of Territorial Systems' (MuSST) programme aims at creating a national museum system. It was established by the Directorate General Museums in the DPCM No. 171 of 29 August 2014, as part of the MiBACT re-organisation, with the aim of initiating a dialogue between public and private museums and encouraging regional museums to present innovative proposals in partnership with other MiBACT institutes, as well as cultural, educational, third sector and private sector organisations.

The MuSST programme is therefore oriented to provide operational support for integration strategies and to encourage the development of best practices for cultural and tourism development, with a view to the shared enhancement of all resources representing the identity of a particular region. In this sense, one of the MuSST objectives is to create a 'practice community' for sharing design expertise and to establish a repertoire of good practices to provide significant indicators for research and operations. In 2016, the Directorate General allocated 500,000 euros to support the projects presented by the regional museum poles, while the second iteration of the programme, entitled 'Cultural Heritage and Local Development Projects', was launched in July 2017 with an overall funding pot of 510,000 euros for 17 museum poles to develop strategic plans for regional development.

The 'Musei Dinamici' project was born out of a collaboration between the Directorate General for Museums of the Ministry of Cultural Heritage and Activities (MiBACT) and the Milan Polytechnic. It was based on the creation of an innovative tool for cultural operators to realise the potential of museums by associating character, personality and behaviour to cultural desires and transforming objects, places and events into instruments of knowledge, participation and emotion for each visitor. The visitor/user to whom the instrument is provided is called to become an active and participatory subject through the expression of his or her own desires. Using neurobiological aspects that connect to logical and emotional models, the instrument uses a computer program to generate customised museum itineraries that are intuitive and easy to use. Drawing on the analysis and advice of museum curators, the itineraries suggest a path for visitors to follow that align with the regional cultural bid. The project, which aims at improving the visitor experience, has been tested at the Maritime Museum of Camogli, the Museum of the Great War of San Colombano, the Museum of Natural History of Milano, the Museum of Design of Milano, the National Archaeological Museum of Altino, the National Archaeological Museum of the Marche, the National Archaeological Museum of Egnazia, the National Archaeological Museum of Ferrara and the National Archaeological Museum of Sibartide – all with excellent results in terms of the feedback received by operators and visitors.

Beyond the abovementioned programmes launched by MiBACT in recent years, several others deserve mention, including a programme aimed at overcoming architectural, cognitive and sensorial barriers and thus increasing access to cultural heritage sites; a programme aimed at enhancing and integrating scientific museums into the national museum system; and a programme aimed at increasing the performance of state museums in the digital environment, strengthening the technological aspect of communication with the aim of enhancing cultural heritage at the national and international levels. In addition to funding these individual programmes, which do not suffice to provide a comprehensive overview of the total set of proposed and ongoing projects,[6] the MiBACT grants provide annual or multi-annual funding to proprietors, owners and managers of individual cultural assets for ordinary and extraordinary conservation, maintenance, restoration and enhancement activities.

Despite the efforts made at local and central levels by experts and technicians, the profound structural and organisational reform of MiBACT (as enacted by DPCM No. 171 of 2014), the increase in 'cultural patronage', the simplification of administrative-bureaucratic procedures and managerial innovation in certain areas of competence (DL 83/2014), and in spite of the exceptional and unique nature of Italy's artistic, environmental and cultural patrimony, it is possible to affirm that Italy does current not adequately valorise its extraordinary patrimony – particularly in comparison to the past or to other countries (e.g. Spain), today. Most likely falling victim to the paradox of abundance, Italy, despite being surrounded by extraordinary environmental, artistic and cultural wealth, does not invest adequately in its cultural assets; rather, the competitive potential of these assets is underestimated, and there is no long-term industrial policy for the sustainable valorisation of the nation's environmental and cultural tourist attractions. The paradox of abundance, of which Italy may be said to fall victim to, is also explained by the negative correlation between a nation's number of UNESCO World Heritage Sites and its investments (relative to GDP) in those heritage assets. Specifically, the data show that nations with fewer World Heritage Sites invest the most in their heritage assets; Italy, as already mentioned, has more World Heritage Sites (53) than any other nation in the world.

It is strategically important for nations to develop a long-term industrial policy to enhance their peculiarities and competitive advantages; from the foregoing, it is evident that cultural heritage is one of the main sectors in which Italy has a global competitive advantage. As mentioned, Italy is endowed with an abundance of heritage assets and beauty; recall that tourism inflows are a form of import that can trigger multiplicative income mechanisms, similar to any traded commodity. The development of a long-term industrial policy based on the sustainable valorisation of tourism in Italy's environmental, artistic and cultural heritage, to be activated through precise and courageous political choices at national and community levels with appropriate financial investments, would activate virtuous and lasting multiplicative mechanisms generating income and wealth over time. The Italian heritage has characteristics of immateriality that, similar to all intangible resources, is difficult to replicate. In the modern world, in which scientific research is able to replicate any product or technology, thereby shortening life cycles and accelerating the obsolescence of products and managerial models, environmental, artistic and cultural heritage is impossible to replicate. The natural beauty and charm surrounding museums, caves and places of historical-archaeological interest, for instance, make the life cycle of these assets infinitely longer and more sustainable. However, in Italy, no beneficial results of these heritage assets will be generated without investment, planning and a true industrial policy, as is particularly evident when we compare Italy with Spain, which profits significantly more from its assets than does Italy.

According to estimates by Cassa depositi e prestiti (2016), international tourism revenues in Spain are more than 40% higher than those in Italy, amounting to approximately 1.5 billion dollars per UNESCO site (compared to less than 1 billion for Italy). It is therefore estimated that, if Italy were to adopt Spanish valuation standards, it would likely see a delta of tourist returns to the value of more than 26 billion euros per year. According to UN data, in 2017, with 82 million tourists declared (representing a 9% increase over the prior year), Spain held the sceptre as the preferred tourist destination over Italy.

In Spain, the average expenditure per foreign tourist is approximately 1,000 euros, generating approximately 49 billion in annual foreign tourist revenue; in Italy, the average expenditure of each foreign tourist is approximately 700 euros, generating a total revenue volume of approximately 34 billion per year. According to data from the World Tourism Organization (2015), compared to a global compound annual growth rate of 6.9% for international tourist spending in the decade 2005–2014, international tourist spending in Italy over the same period grew by only 2.8%, with an obvious negative repercussion on average tourist spending. In this decade, in which luxury became a tourist driver, Italy seems to have slipped in the international rankings of popularity, revealing its extreme difficulty in intercepting the most affluent tourists, despite its extraordinary history and modern appeal in the sense of evocative brands, style and fashion.

Returning to the comparison with Spain, as highlighted by Cassa depositi e prestiti (2016), one of the drivers of Spanish tourism is undoubtedly Spain's wide-ranging national planning for the tourism sector, which gives great attention to strategic planning and operational implementation. The Plan of the Tourism Espanol Horizonte 2020, in addition to defining the objectives and strategy for developing Spanish tourism, also outlines an operative plan for the implementation and realisation of the interventions across various sub-periods. In 2012, the national tourism plan was launched – the Plan Nacional and Integral de Turismo (PNIT) – for the 2012–2015 time horizon, aimed at strengthening the role of Spain as a leading country in world tourism through reviving the Spanish brand, developing tourist loyalty and improving the procedures for issuing visas; it also included initiatives aimed at reducing the seasonality of tourism. Of particular interest, Spain used these plans to launch a national project, drawing on a clear and well-communicated industrial policy, selling itself to potential tourists, enhancing the effectiveness of its online portal (www.spain.info) and improving the image of not only tourism in Spain, but also the entire country, generating a positive impact on national wealth, production and employment.

Considering the previously highlighted data and the growth expectations for world tourism (especially from Chinese tourists) in the coming years, it is evident how profitable it is – at both public and private levels – to invest in tourism, also considering the low remuneration rates that, today, guarantee many alternative investments. In order to attract foreign capital and investors, however, certain infrastructural bases must be developed through investment, planning and policy making. Unfortunately, in Italy, none of these actions are guaranteed. The funds spent by the Italian government for cultural heritage are inadequate and in constant and continuous decline; furthermore, they are largely destined for protection and conservation acts, and only minimally for valorisation. Therefore, Italy demonstrates a defensive, prudent and short-sighted vision that is not oriented to long-term investment. What is missing in Italy, as we have said, is a synergistic and long-term industrial policy based on the sustainable valorisation of the nation's environmental, artistic and cultural heritage, substantiated through a supply chain consisting of regional strategic planning, attention to environmental sustainability, investment in research and development, logistics, the redevelopment of degraded urban environments, links between international hubs and heritage assets, process and product innovation, tools for business combinations, financing projects, public–private partnerships and integrated and synergistic promo-marketing.

In this sense, the comparison with Spain appears even more ruthless than previously outlined, especially considering the bi-annual indicator of international tourism competitiveness published by the World Economic Forum (WEF). Through this indicator, the WEF aims at comparing nations on a series of factors and policies, divided into 14 'pillars' that facilitate the sustainable development of the travel and tourism industry. In the WEF report, the Travel and Tourism Competitiveness Index (TTCI) compares the tourism economies of 136 countries around the world; in 2017, Spain was ranked 1st, followed by France and Germany, while Italy was ranked 8th. Through an analysis of the WEF report, it is interesting to analyse the determining factors of national tourism competitiveness and, consequently, national tourism weaknesses. As highlighted earlier, Italy is significantly lacking in competitiveness relative to other nations in terms of context factors (i.e. the business environment, human resources and the labour market, information and communications technology and overall infrastructure). This is mainly due to low bureaucratic efficiency (in which Italy is ranked 134th out of 136 countries) and an excessive tax impact on investment incentives (in which Italy is ranked 135th out of 136). Italy also falls significantly behind other European nations with respect to policies implemented to support tourism development – a proxy of national strategic foresight, public spending for the sector and the effectiveness of tourism marketing. This lack of attention to organising and equipping the nation in such a way as to be able to receive tourists in an optimal manner inevitably affects the indicator of environmental sustainability, for which Italy ranks the lowest among all nations. After all, where tourist pressure is badly managed, the tension between tourism and the environment becomes immediately evident. Therefore, the WEF report presents Italy as a nation that wastes its extraordinary wealth of artistic, cultural and environmental heritage because it does not sufficiently invest in its enhancement and promotion: it does not use modern branding and marketing, it does not provide adequate incentives to encourage businesses in tourism, it does not engage in long-term planning or infrastructure investments and it gags the private and public entrepreneurial spirit with disproportionate, inefficient and therefore useless and harmful bureaucracy.

Wealth management in the art sector

Over the last decade, the proportion of works of art in the managed portfolios of private customers at the international level has progressively increased, due to the low rates of return guaranteed by traditional asset classes and from the need for portfolio managers to look for alternative classes of assets that guarantee higher returns as well as greater diversification of the managed portfolios. At the same time, specialised investment funds for works of art have also increased, particularly since 2004, when the first investment fund of the Fine Art Group was launched. Today, the Fine Art Group is a world leader in portfolio management and financial consulting for the art sector.[7] Since its launch in 2004, similar funds have emerged with the result that, now, investors looking to invest in art can choose from a wide variety of investment funds from different management companies. It is estimated that this growth trend is destined to continue into the next decade, as the value invested in art and collectibles from 'ultra-high-net-worth individuals' (UHNWI)[8] (which in 2016 amounted to 1,600 billion dollars) is expected to reach the 2,700 billion dollars mark by 2026 (Deloitte, 2017).

Similar to jewels, vintage wines and vintage cars, works of art belong to the asset class of collectibles and can be defined as emotional assets because they inspire an emotional reaction in the investor linked to the pleasure of owning them.[9] In more detail, it is possible to segment the asset class of works of art into the following categories: ancient visual art, modern visual art, contemporary (i.e. post-war) art, pre-Columbian art, photography, sculpture, old books, prints and engravings. It is therefore evident that the artistic asset class is characterised by a high degree of heterogeneity and a lack of internal comparability, as it consists of unique products that cannot be compared in terms of intrinsic characteristics and markets (Fandella, 2018).

Over the 15-year period between 2002 and 2017, the main art market indexes developed by Artnet recorded positive annual returns of between 1.54% and 14.1% in the market for contemporary art and, especially, Chinese contemporary art, which records the highest average growth. In general, during this period, the main indices of the art market recorded an average satisfactory performance – in many cases, better than the indexes of the main companies listed on the international list, but also a more volatile performance due to the lack of a historical consolidation price that leaves many of the art markets subject to speculative trends (Deloitte, 2017).

Data from the last 15 years suggest that investing in art is profitable but, on average, riskier than investing in equity securities of the main listed companies, due to a higher average investment volatility. Investing in art, however, enables investors to diversify their portfolio beyond traditional financial instruments, as shown by the low average correlation rates between the art market indices and the S&P 500 and Euros Stoxx 50 indices; subsequently, this reduces the overall risk of the portfolio. Also for this reason, the percentage of investment in art in the portfolios of UHNWI investors at the international level has progressively increased in recent years.

In fact, as regards 'noble' buying reasons, collectors have always acquired works of art essentially for emotional reasons and to obtain social consensus; however, in recent years, financial convenience and the need for portfolio diversification have become more important determinants of purchase patterns, and this makes the collector an ideal customer for the wealth management sector. Individuals who buy works of art are hardly speculators oriented to the short term, but collectors or investors seeking to qualify, diversify, increase and manage their assets over a medium- to long-term time horizon, acquiring assets that are comparable to shelter assets, which maintain value over time and also involve emotional value. Development of the art market therefore generates increased demand for professional financial services linked to wealth management and insurance. According to Deloitte,[10] therefore, a large majority of collectors buy art not only for passion, but also for investment, with the aim of diversifying and consolidating their portfolio. This widens the wealth management market to include new asset classes and types of investors; accordingly, the market develops new services, such as (but not limited to) support for the valuation of works of art, art insurance, art advising, periodic reporting and tax planning, value protection and risk management in the art sector, management of portfolios that include works of art, financing works of art, inheritance succession and philanthropy. In particular, operators in the art sector and art collectors express a need for more advice on the subject of authentication, assessment and the development of works of art, in a market that is still not transparent not very liquid and at high risk for counterfeiting and, in general, fraudulent behaviour.

These demands appear more felt today, also because of the dizzying growth of online transactions of works of art. According to the 2017 Hiscox Online Art Trade report, online sales of art goods reached an estimated value of 3.75 billion dollars in 2016 (+15% compared to 2015). In particular, Sotheby's increased its online business by 19% and Christies by 34% in 2016. Today, online auctions represent approximately 8.4% of the total auction market and follow a growth trend. There are, therefore, significant opportunities for development with respect to new, specialised and high value-added services in the area of art wealth management.[11]

From the demand perspective, the development of financial services linked to the art world enables greater coverage of both the real and potential financial needs of investors; on the supply side, such development of new services facilitates a holistic approach to total asset management for customers, which is fundamental in the sector (which is particularly attentive to the quality and completeness of the services offered, amidst increasing competitive pressure). A fundamental component of the offer is represented by investment funds, which, together with trusts, represent the main instrument for managing assets that invest in works of art. Unlike trusts, which represent a closed instrument for managing works of art that are exclusively owned by the same settlor, investment funds aim at investing the assets of a plurality of investors with the objective of generating profit. As mentioned, since the launch in 2004 of the first investment fund for works of art (i.e. the Fine Art Fund), the market for investment funds that invest part of their heritage in art has greatly expanded. Although it is not possible to provide a precise number of such funds – because many are not listed and even their disclosure does not allow for an exhaustive examination of their investments – there are now more than 20 funds that definitely invest assets in the contemporary art sector. Almost half of these funds are located in the United Kingdom (five funds, of which four are offshoots of the Fine Art Group) and Luxembourg (five funds); there are also three US funds and others based in offshore markets such as Malta, Gibraltar, Israel, San Marino and the Cayman Islands.[12]

Notes

1 For more on the use of project financing to fund heritage assets, please see Miller (2006); Licciardi and Rana (2012); Leardini, Rossi and Moggi (2014); Tardivo, Battisti and Riorda (2015); Besana and Esposito (2016); Bevilacqua, Bianchi, Calvani and Rovai (2016); Carè (2018).
2 For more information on the technical characteristics of the project financing instrument with respect to heritage assets, reference is made, *inter alia*, to Lettieri (2009); Libanora (2011); Nicolai (2011); Mariani, Menaldi and Associati (2012); Gatti (2013); Finnerty (2013); Sambri (2014); Tinsley (2014); Spagnuolo (2017); Montani (2018); Pietrantonio (2018).
3 For a more in-depth analysis of the use of the business plan in the financing of heritage assets, please refer to, among others, Bishoff and Allen (2004); Luisiani and Zan (2010); Donohoe (2012); Montelli (2012); Brunelli (2014); Laing, Wheeler, Reeves and Warwick (2014); Kalman (2014); Hill (2016); Romão, Paupério and Pereora (2016).
4 On the other hand, in order to examine the technical features of the business plan instrument more generally (not linked to the financing of heritage assets), please refer to Borello (2012); Di Toma (2012); Donatelli and Schultz (2012); Mariani (2012); Mariani (2013); Brusa (2016); Finch (2016); Cardoni (2018); domenico (2018); Lolli (2018).
5 ROI constitutes the profitability quotient of company activity, regardless of the accessory, financial, extraordinary and tax effects of management. Improvement in ROI over a period of several years indicates improvement in the company's operating efficiency.
6 For further information on programmes and funding measures, please see the MiBACT website, where details on the programmes outlined in this section can be found.
7 The founder and current CEO of the Fine Art Group is Phillip Hoffman, creator of the first investment fund in art and the subsequent funds of the Fine Art Group, and formerly financial director and deputy director of Christie's Europe.

8 The term "high-net-worth individuals' (HNWI) is commonly used in the world of finance (particularly in private banking) and luxury to indicate individuals with a high net worth. Although there is no single definition of such persons, individuals whose net global assets exceed $30 million are typically included in this category, according to a taxonomy created by Cap Gemini-Merril Lynch. The global HNWI population is constantly growing: 2016 showed an increase of 3.5% on the previous year, and a growth of 46% is expected on an aggregate basis by 2026. It is evident that the growth of the HNWI population has significantly impacted the market for collectibles, given that, on average, HNWI invest approximately 4% of their portfolio in such assets.

9 On the subject of emotional assets, see, for example Boido and Ceccherini (2018).

10 See Deloitte (various years). *Art & finance report*. Deloitte Luxembourg & ArtTactic.

11 For a closer look at the business management sector, see Musile Tanzi (2007); Liu, Zan and Guo (2008); Varbanova (2013); Paquette and Redaelli (2015); Ragazzoni and Zanaboni (2015); Zorloni (2016); Devereaux (2018).

12 For further information on the various art funds in the international market, see Fandella (2018).

References

Besana A., Esposito A. (2016), "Understanding Economics and Marketing of Ecomuseums: An Exploration of a USA Sample", in *Business Challenges in the Changing Economic Landscape – Vol. 2 – Proceedings of the 14th Eurasia Business and Economics Society Conference* (Edited by) Bilgin, M.H., Danis, H., Demir, E., Can, U, Springer, Berlino.

Bevilacqua M.G., Bianchi L., Calvani C., Rovai M. (2016), "The recovery of the Italian industrial heritage: the case of the Solvay Silos by Pier Luigi Nervi in San Vincenzo (Tuscany)", in *World Heritage and Degradation: Smart Design, Planning and Technologies*, Proceedings of *Le vie dei Mercanti. XIV Forum Internazionale di Studi*, La scuola di Pitagora, Napoli.

Bishoff L., Allen N. (2004), *Business Planning for Cultural Heritage Institutions – A framework and resource guide to assist cultural heritage institutions with business planning for sustainability of digital asset management programs*, Council on Library and Information Resources, Washington, DC.

Boido C., Ceccherini P. (2018), "Investimenti alternativi: Gli emotional assets", in *Rivista Bancaria – Minerva Bancaria*, n. 1/2018.

Borello A. (2012), *Il business plan, dalla valutazione dell'investimento alla misurazione dell'attività d'impresa*, New York: McGraw Hill.

Brunelli M. (2014), *Heritage interpretation: un nuovo approccio per l'educazione al patrimonio*, Macerata: Edizioni Università di Macerata 2014.

Brusa L. (2016), *Business plan: guida per imprese sane, start-up e aziende in crisi*, Egea, Milano.

Cardoni A. (2018), "Strategic planning for value creation in business networks: Conceptual framework and theoretical proposals", in *Management control – Franco Angeli*, n.1/2018.

Carè R. (2018), "Being a Sustainable Bank: The Case of Intesa Sanpaolo", in *Sustainable Banking – Issues and Challenges*, (a cura di) Carè R., Springer, Berlino.

Deloitte, Art & Finance Report, various years, Deloitte Luxembourg & ArtTactic.

Devereaux C. (2018), *Arts and Cultural Management: Sense and Sensibilities in the State of the Field,* Routledge, Londra.

Di Toma P. (2012), "Il business plan: Le analisi di sensitività per la valutazione dei risultati", in *Bilancio, vigilanza e controlli – Euroconference* n.10/2012.

Di Toma P. (2012), "Il business plan: Le analisi di sensitività per la valutazione dei risultati", in *Bilancio, vigilanza e controlli – Euroconference* n.10/2012.

Domenico N. (2018), "Carenze informative e vulnerabilità delle imprese giovani del business plan", in *Management control – Franco Angeli*, n. 2/2018.

Donohoe H.M. (2012), "Sustainable heritage tourism marketing and Canada's Rideau Canal world heritage site", in *Journal of Sustainable Tourism – Routledge*, n. 20/ 2012.

Fandella P. (2018), "Lo sviluppo dei Fondi in arte come opportunità di diversificazione del portafoglio di investimento", in *Rivista Bancaria Minerva Bancaria*, n. 2–3/2018.

Finch B. (2016), *How to write a business plan*, Kogan Plan, London.

Finnerty J.D. (2013), *Project financing: Asset-based financial engineering*, Hoboken, NJ: Wiley.

Gatti S. (2013), *Project Finance in Theory and Practice: Designing, Structuring, and Financing Private and Public Projects*, Amsterdam: Academic Press.

Hill S. (2016), "Constructive conservation – a model for developing heritage assets", in *Journal of Cultural Heritage Management and Sustainable Development – Emerald*, n. 6/2016.

Kalman H. (2014), *Heritage Planning. Principles and Process*, London: Taylor & Francis.

Laing J., Wheeler F., Reeves K., Warwick F. (2014), "Assessing the experiential value of heritage assets: A case study of a Chinese heritage precinct, Bendigo, Australia", in *Tourism Management – Elsevier*, n. 40/2014.

Leardini C., Rossi G., Moggi S. (2014), "Outlining Italian Bank Foundations", in *Board Governance in Bank Foundations – The Italian Experience*, (Edited by) Leardini C., Rossi G., Moggi S., Springer Verlag, Berlino.

Lettiere M. (2009), Il *project financing: Disciplina e operatività*, Aracne, Roma.

Libanora M. (2011), *Le società miste pubblico-privato e le operazioni di project financing: Gli strumenti per rilanciare servizi pubblici e investimenti negli enti locali*, Ipsoa, Milanofiori, Assago.

Licciardi G., Rana A. (2012), *The Economics of Uniqueness: Investing in Historic City Cores and Cultural Heritage Assets for Sustainable Development*, Washington, DC: World Bank.

Liu S., Zan L., Guo Y. (2008), *The management of cultural heritage in China: general trends and micro-focus on the Luoyang municipality*, Egea, Milano.

Lolli A. (2018), "Il modello di business di Intesa Sanpaolo nel nuovo piano industriale: The business model of big European player: Intesa Sanpaolo's new strategic plan", in *Bancaria*, n. 74/2018.

Luisiani M., Zan L. (2010), "Institutional transformation and managerialism in cultural heritage: Heritage Malta", in *Museum Management and Curatorship – Taylor & Francis*, n. 25/2010.

Mariani M., Menaldi & Associati, (2012), *Il project financing: Analisi giuridica, economica-finanziaria, tecnica, tributaria, bancaria, assicurativa*, Giappichelli, Torino.

Mariani G. (2012), *Conoscenza e creazione di valore: Il ruolo del business plan*, Franco Angeli, Milano.

Mariani G. (2013), "Conoscere per formulare e comunicare le strategie: Il ruolo del business plan", in *Sinergie: Periodico di studi e ricerche*, 31(2013), n. 92.

Montani V. (2018), *Il project financing: Inquadramento giuridico e logiche manutentive*, Giappichelli, Torino.

Miller S. (2006), "Stakeholders and community participation", in *Managing World Heritage Sites*, (a cura di) Leask A., Fyall A., Amsterdam: Elsevier.

Montelli M. M. (2012), "Marketing del cultural heritage territoriale e musei di impresa: Un caso di analisi", in *Mercati e competitività – Franco Angeli*, n. 3/2012.

Musile Tanzi P. (2007), "Art banking: Opportunità e rischi nel wealth management" in *Bancaria*, n.63/2007.

Nicolai M. (2011), *Finanza pubblica e privata: Incentivi alle imprese, fondi mobiliari e immobiliari, cartolarizzazioni, derivati, project financing, patto di stabilità e federalismo*, Maggioli, Sant'Arcangelo di Romagna (RN).

Paquette J., Redaelli E. (2015), *Arts Management and Cultural Policy Research*, Springer, Berlino.

Pietrantonio L. G. (2018), *Il project financing tra pubblico e privato: Problemi, scenari e prospettive*, Giappichelli, Torino.

Ragazzoni M., Zanaboni B. (2015), *L'art advisory nel private banking: Opportunità e rischi dell'investimento in arte*, AIPB, Milano.

Romão X., Paupério E., Pereora N. (2016), "A framework for the simplified risk analysis of cultural heritage assets", in *Journal of Cultural Heritage – Elsevier*, n. 20/2016.

Sambri S. M. (2014), *Project financing: La finanza di progetto per la realizzazione di opere pubbliche*, CEDAM, Padova.

Spagnuolo M. (2017), *Il Project Financing e il Partenariato Pubblico e Privato*, Simone, Napoli.

Tardivo G., Battisti E., Riorda M. (2015), "Role of financial services and real estate management – towards a new value chain: Exploratory research findings", in *Journal of Financial Management & Analysis*, Vol. 28, Issue 2.

Tinsley R. (2014), *Advanced Project Financing, Structuring Risks*, London: Euromoney Institutional Investor plc.

Varbanova L. (2013), *Strategic Management in the Arts,* Routledge, Londra.

Zorloni A. (2016), *Art Wealth Management: Managing Private Art Collections*, Springer International Publishing, Svizzera.

4 The valuation of heritage assets

Introduction

This chapter addresses the valuation of heritage assets, which is complicated and contentious due to the economic activities of such assets, which generate income to cover their management, protection and storage/conservation costs. The valuation of a cultural or landscape asset can produce an economic value (following an estimation process) or a price (following a negotiation process). As these numbers result from different processes characterised by often dissimilar purposes, they can differ quit widely. For this reason, before moving on to discuss the methodologies used to value heritage assets, the chapter will first explore the significant phenomenon of divergence between the price and value of heritage assets, which are often affected by a lack of comparable assets, due to their characteristic uniqueness.

In this respect, it should be emphasised that the value of a cultural or landscape asset is not merely economic, but also social and cultural; thus, *lato sensu*, it is difficult to measure its true value. Moreover, cultural or socials benefits to a community are difficult to economically quantify; it is also difficult for them to be appropriately reflected and identified in the value or price of the cultural or landscape asset. Notwithstanding these challenges, it seems safe to assume that a public or private entity would be motivated to invest in a given cultural or landscape asset (to secure its protection, preservation or enhancement),[1] as long as the asset is at least potentially able to generate some benefit (be this economic, social, scientific or cultural) for its stakeholders or shareholders.

It appears clear, therefore, that the valuation of heritage assets, however complex and slippery, is of extreme relevance for a multitude of subjects, be they public taxpayers, uninformed local residents, informed public or private investors or administrators of the public or private entities that own a share of the analysed asset. In this respect, it is useful to underline that all heritage assets have the characteristics of immateriality and, similar to most intangible resources, they are hardly replicable because they are unique and different from all other cultural and landscape assets; in this respects, they are unrivalled in the tourist market.

An appropriately protected cultural or landscape asset has the potential to be timeless and not excludible, because it is not easy – ethically speaking – to prevent persons from enjoying its wealth. This characteristic of heritage assets, which makes their economic appraisal so complex, also makes their investment potentially profitable, particularly when the income generated from the asset is able to compensate for the costs incurred in managing, protecting and conserving the asset.

In the modern world, in which scientific research is able to replicate any product or technology, thereby shortening life cycles and accelerating the obsolescence of products and managerial models, cultural and landscape assets are impossible to replicate. The natural beauty and charm surrounding museums, caves and historical-archaeological landmarks, for instance, make the life cycle of these assets infinitely longer and more sustainable. Investors in cultural assets can therefore reasonably aim at earning a stable and lasting return on their investment, however hard this might be to measure *ex ante*. These investors are likely to also activate a multiplicative intergenerational process of development, because their investment may contribute to securing the availability of the protected asset for future generations and add value to the country in which the asset is located. In other words, investment in the protection, conservation and valorisation of a cultural or landscape asset may trigger a virtuous circle, improving public visibility for the asset and stimulating further public and private redevelopment and restoration of the surrounding environment. In this way, investment may create opportunities for territorial development that activate other multiplicative mechanisms involving income and value.

It should be clarified that the objective of the present chapter is not to separate the valuation of heritage assets from their economic management, but to differentiate the valuation of the private or public entities that manage the assets. Therefore, in the chapter we do not discuss valuation models for cultural or landscape assets *stricto sensu*, but explore the models used to value the companies that manage these heritage assets.

Price versus value of heritage assets

The process of valuation uses comprehensive estimation to attribute a value to a company's economic capital.[2] The economic capital of a company that manages a heritage asset, similar to any other company, is comprised by all of its production factors, be these tangible or intangible. The numbers attached to the value and the price of a company's economic capital often conspicuously diverge, as they result from two very different processes: the value is the result of an estimate, while the price is the result of a negotiation. In the first case, economic capital value is obtained using income forecasts and assessment of a company's risk level. In the second case, economic capital price is obtained from a market negotiation between representatives of the supply and representatives of the demand for economic capital ownership (assuming the company that manages the asset is trading in the market).

Furthermore, in the case of heritage assets, significant differences between price and value are often influenced by the lack of trading markets for similar or comparable assets, on account of the uniqueness that characterises such assets.

Generally speaking, the processes of valuing a company's economic capital versus setting its price (through negotiation) are characterised by:

- different targets;
- different projection horizons;
- different schemes and logical criteria adopted by the traders; and
- different relevant variables.

As a result of these differences, the two processes often produce divergent results, even though they are closely related.

The valuation of a company's economic capital is a complex process aimed at estimating the company's income production capacity over a medium-to long-term projection horizon (generally the assumed company lifetime). Notwithstanding the differences amongst the many valuation methods we will elaborate in this chapter, the economic capital value is a function of the relationship between potential income generation and a specific discount rate, which is chosen to reflect the company's perceived (by its stakeholders) level of risk.

In the process of valuing the economic capital of a company managing a heritage asset, a number of variables – both internal and external to the company – must be considered. Among the internal variables, the following may be noted:

- the artistic and environmental uniqueness of the heritage asset managed, and its resultant social, cultural and economic value;
- potential and additional capital endowment, both tangible and intangible, provided by the managing company;
- potential and additional availability of incidental and secondary tourist attractions that could compete with the heritage asset and generate income;
- the accessibility and usability of the heritage asset;
- the connections between national and international hubs and the heritage asset;
- the quality and logistics of the urban environment of the heritage asset;
- past economic performance of the managing company;
- qualifying expertise of the managing company staff;
- trends in use of the heritage asset over recent years;
- the managing company's ability to valorise the heritage asset;

- the satisfaction and customer experience of visitors to the heritage asset; and
- the possibility of creating tourist trails and an integrated and diversified tourist service around the heritage asset.

External variables may include:

- cyclical variables related to current/expected economic conditions (i.e. expansion vs. slump);
- global tourist trends for the country in which the heritage asset is located;
- global art sector trends relating to the prices of works owned by public and private entities;
- specific risks linked to the country (e.g. terrorism, political instability and environmental hazards); and
- the risk of new market entrants that would imitate the heritage asset or offer an alternative touristic attraction.

All of the abovementioned variables – both internal and external – must be analysed in the valuation process, because they are all able to influence the economic value of the managing company. The variables also apply to the negotiation process, because both representatives of demand and representatives of supply (i.e. stock ownership) base their investment/divestment decisions on their own assessments of economic capital value. Despite this, however, there are significant differences between the two processes. The decision to trade shares in a listed company may be driven by several motivations, including:

- to obtain or divest company control;
- to hold (or sell) stock in the company over a medium- to long-term horizon; and
- to attain speculative or hedging and arbitraging goals.

Behind each of these motivations lies a different logical process and a different estimation method for valuing the stock or share. Given this variation in investors' objectives (in terms of targets, time horizons and logical schemes), their processes of valuating and negotiating a company's economic capital may also generate different results.

Finally, the difference between economic capital value and price can also be attributable to external variables that are relevant in the negotiation process but not considered in the assessment of economic capital. Such variables include:

- the efficiency of financial markets at the time when the company is listed on the stock exchange;[3]
- the presence of transitional costs;

- the cyclical development of the supply/demand of venture capital and the cyclical development of financial markets;
- the earnings of potential investors and their propensity to invest (often influenced by extra-economic factors that are difficult to measure and weight); and
- concentration processes in the company's sector or operating area (Guatri and Bini, 2005: 13).

Fundamental analysis and the family method of valuating companies that manage heritage assets

As conveyed previously, the aim of this chapter is not to separate the valuation of heritage assets from their economic management, but to differentiate the valuation of companies (both private and public) that manage such assets.

For this reason, we do not discuss models used to value cultural or landscape assets *strictu sensu*, but instead describe the models used to value companies that manage heritage assets. In this regard, it is necessary to start with fundamental analysis, which consists of the evaluation of summary and prospective data and data on the macroeconomic framework, economic sectors and corporate accounts. This analytical method is largely used to determine a company's economic, financial and patrimonial net worth.

In the fundamental analysis of a company, evaluation of the macro-economic framework is based on an analysis and estimate of international economic conditions, macroeconomic variables (e.g. GDP, inflation rates, productive investments, technological innovation, account and trade balances, employment, interest rates, exchange rates, public debt, etc.) and the traders' expectations of economic, monetary and fiscal policy development.

After an assessment of the macroeconomic framework, the relevant economic sectors of the company of interest are analysed to identify sectoral opportunities and risks. Following this, the analysis moves to the valuation of the particular company under assessment.

The valuation of a company aims at defining the value of its economic capital (also referred to as 'fair value'), regardless of its actual market price at the time. In this analysis, it is assumed that a company's economic capital comprises all of its assets – both tangible and intangible – in a single unity. In other words, to estimate a company's economic capital, we maximise its capacity by combining all of its factors efficiently to assess future income. Immediately, we may note that this valuation process involves a range of discretionary choices; this is because the process involves prediction based on current information, which is often incomplete. In particular, the incompleteness of sources may lead to deficient corporate disclosure with respect to intangibles, which are crucial for the economic performance of companies managing heritage assets. The process of evaluating a company's economic capital thus produces varying estimates, depending on:

- the skills and professionalism of the assessor;
- the discretionary choices of the assessor, in terms of both the assessment model used and the incorporation of particular model variables;
- the available information and the information taken into account.

Therefore, valuation of a company's economic capital can hardly be counted on to generate a single replicable result. For most companies – and in particular those that manage a heritage asset – the methods used to determine economic capital value are as follows:[4]

- asset capital methods;
- income methods;
- mixed asset-income methods;
- financial methods; and
- empirical methods (i.e. use of multiples).

Capital asset methods estimate a company's economic capital value in terms of its tangible and intangible properties. Such methods express the market value of all assets listed in the balance sheet, as well as corporate intangibles that are otherwise unaccounted for. The aim of these methods is to define the value of adjusted equity that can be considered a company's economic capital. In this family of valuation methods, we can distinguish simple patrimonial approaches from complex capital approaches, according to whether corporate intangibles are assessed. In simple capital approaches, adjusted equity (K) is generally estimated by means of formulations similar to that presented below:

$$K = C + \left(\sum_{i=1}^{n} P_i - \sum_{i=1}^{n} M_i \right) * (1 - r)$$

Where:
K = adjusted equity;
C = equity accounting;
P_i = capital gains (calculated over the projection horizon (i) from '1' to 'n');
M_i = capital losses (calculated over the projection horizon (i) from '1' to 'n'); and
r = the tax burden, calculated on the basis of the current tax rate.

In complex capital approaches, however, the company's intangible assets are also taken into account. This approach seems particularly appropriate for companies that manage heritage assets.

Therefore, it is possible to estimate adjusted equity ('K') using complex capital approaches by correcting the estimates produced from simple approaches, as follows:

$$K' = K + 1 * (1 - r)$$

Where:
K' = adjusted net worth, assessed using complex capital approaches;
K = adjusted equity, assessed using simple capital approaches;
I = intangibles assets, assessed using appropriate valuation methodologies;[5] and
r = the tax burden, calculated on the basis of the current tax rate.

However, by considering a company's simple aggregate of assets, capital methods – both simple and complex – have the limitation of expressing an economic capital value that does not include a company's earnings prospects and does not consider management efficiency or the company's level of risk.

Furthermore, in the case of companies that manage heritage assets, these methodologies encounter the challenges and limitations inherent in cultural and landscape asset valuation. Taken in isolation, they appear unsuitable to fully and appropriately assess the economic capital value of such a company.

Income methods, in contrast, estimate company value by discounting the income that the company expects to generate over time. Such methods require a forecast of average income, an appropriate discount rate and a projection horizon.

The forecast of average income 'R' can be determined by adjusting – according to the company's future prospects – a representative indicator of past financial performance.

Depending on the type of income considered for the estimation, an appropriate discount rate should be determined (actualisation). The discount rate 'I', defining the company's own capital, reflects the level of risk relating to the forecasted income.

The projection horizon refers to the period for which it is justifiable to assume that the company will be capable of generating income. On account of the difficultly of making this determination, it is usually assumed to be unlimited. Through the use of income methods, therefore, the calculation of economic capital value is essentially the current value of a perpetual annuity (constant instalment) R, discounted at rate I; thus, the company's value is R/i.

Income methods, although often excessively synthetic in their formulation and thus less clear and testable, are the most suitable for estimating the economic capital value of companies managing heritage assets. These methods focus on cash or income flows, which they adjust according to the corporate risk level. They also consider specificities related to the cultural or landscape asset managed and, in this way, estimate the company's capacity to enhance managed worth without walking the slippery and arduous path of patrimonial valuation of the particular heritage asset.

Mixed asset-income methods consider both equity and income when estimating a company's economic capital value. Through these methodologies, the resulting company value is assumed to reflect both current conditions (adjusted equity worth) and future earnings (forecasted conditions). Therefore, the methods involve a ratified valuation of adjusted equity according to the company's capacity to generate income that is above or below average yield for the sector.[6] Company value is thus estimated as adjusted equity, corrected for the yield spread that the company is able to generate, compared to the sector's average profitability.

Identifying 'Rmp' as perspective average income, 'K' as adjusted equity and 'r' as the average rate of return of the specific sector, the company's yield spread 'D' is given by:

$$D = R_{mp} - K*r$$

It is therefore necessary to determinate the value of this spread, considering an unlimited time horizon and a discount rate 'i', which reflects the company's risk level. The company's goodwill, 'G' (or, when negative, badwill), is thus given by the following formula:

$$G = (R_{mp} - K*r)/i$$

The company's economic capital value is obtained by adding the value of adjusted equity, corrected by the attribution of goodwill (or badwill):

Financial methods valuate a company's economic capital value by discounting the cash flows it is expected to generate over time. As the cash flows considered in this assessment change, the discount rate (or discounting) should also change, in reflection of the level of risk connected to the expected cash flows.

The underlying assumption of these methodologies is that a company's value stems from its cash flows and that it will be able to sustain these cash flows over time.

Accordingly, a company's value can be summarised with the following formula:

$$\text{Economic value} = \sum_{t-1}^{n} \frac{FC_t}{(1+i)^t}$$

Where:

FC_t = cash flows generated by the company through the management of a heritage asset at time t and added over the projection horizon; and

I = the discount rate.

With regard to the ability of these methodologies to estimate the economic capital value of a company that manages heritage assets, the same argument may be applied as previously presented with regard to income methods.

Finally, in valuations using multiples, economic capital value is empirically derived from the price or value of comparable companies on the basis of common variables such as earnings, cash flows or net worth.

A typical example of such a valuation approach draws on an average sector index price/net equity (or price/earnings). These methods assume that other companies in the sector are comparable to the company being evaluated and that the market provides an appropriate assessment.

In the case of companies that manage heritage assets, this family of valuation methods is inadequate because of the uniqueness of the assets managed. For this reason, other companies in the sector are not necessarily comparable.

Methods of valuating heritage assets

The previous section introduced the primary categories of methods used to valuate companies that manage heritage assets. The present section now moves to describe four methods used to valuate heritage assets. With respect to the previous methodologies discussed, the below should be understood as complementary, rather than alternative, methods.[7]

The methodologies discussed are as follows:

- a market approach that identifies, under certain circumstances, asset value according to the equilibrium price derived in the free market trading between the public or private owner of the asset (interested in divesting; i.e. the bidder) and a public or private player willing to acquire the asset (i.e. the asker);
- an economic method that estimates asset value according to the summary and prospective measurement of the economic value that is created or destroyed by the public or private body that manages the asset;
- a financial method based on discounting the cash flows generated by the asset (i.e. its tourist or usage value) and discounting the public or private investment for its protection, conservation or enhancement (i.e. its intrinsic value); and
- a qualitative method drawing on the professional opinions of a group of independent and anonymous experts, building on the so-called 'Delphi method'.

Market approach

In some methods of valuating heritage assets, it is considered appropriate to start with the equilibrium price formed in the free market trading between the public or private owner seeking to transfer the asset (i.e. the bidder) and the public or private entity who is willing to buy it (i.e. the asker), assuming perfect information symmetry between parties and no extra-economic factors that could alter the parties' propensity for trading.[8]

According to the law of supply and demand, the exchange should occur at the moment when the demand curve intercepts the supply curve. In order to determine the price at this equilibrium (P segnato), two variables must be calculated: the maximum price that the asker is willing to pay (P_{MaxD}) and the minimum price required by the bidder (P_{MinO}).

The equation used to identify P_{MaxD} is expressed as follows:

$$P_{MaxD} = \sum_{i=1}^{n} \frac{R_i}{(1+r_d)^i} - \frac{C_i}{(1+r_d)^i}$$

Where:

P_{MaxD} = the maximum price the asker is willing to pay;

R_i = an estimate of the revenues generated by asset up to time 'i' (i-esimo), summed for the projection horizon;

C_i = an estimate of the overall costs necessary for maintaining, conserving, managing, promoting and enhancing the asset up to time 'i', summed for the projection horizon; and

r_d = the discount rate that reflects the investor's minimum expected return (i.e. the opportunity cost).

From this, it is assumed that the equilibrium price (P segnato) is included within the set of whole values bounded above by P_{MaxD} and below by P_{MinO} [P_{MinO}; P_{MaxD}]. In other words, if an opportunity were to arise for the buyer to obtain the asset at a lower price than the maximum price that he or she would be willing to spend, his or her utility function would be expressed through the following formulation:

$$U_d : P_{MaxD} - \overline{P}$$

Where:

U_d = the utility function of demand, expressed as the opportunity for the asker to acquire the asset at a lower price than the maximum price he or she is willing to pay;

P_{MaxD}: the maximum price that the asker is willing to pay; and
P segnato: the equilibrium price.

Conversely, from the bidder's perspective, if the opportunity were to arise to sell the asset at a higher price than minimum price that he or she was available to accept, his or her utility function (UI) would be assessed through the following formulation:

$$U_o = \bar{P} - P_{MinO}$$

Where:
U = the utility function of supply;
P segnato: the equilibrium price; and
P_{Min}: the minimum price required by the bidder.

In order to indicate this more clearly, the utility function of supply (U) should be considered through two alternative hypotheses.

In the first hypothesis, the asset under discussion is able to produce a net income under its current conditions; therefore, by selling it, the bidder incurs some loss of future revenues, quantifiable as the estimated cumulative income over a predefined time horizon, discounted at a rate that reflects the business risk. Such estimations will naturally be assessed by the seller in the process of determining his or her minimum price (P_{MinU}). In the second hypothesis, the asset under discussion is unable to produce a net income under its current conditions; therefore, it is no loss of revenues is associated with its sale.

However, it is appropriate to also consider costs related to the asset's conservation and maintenance, which are further associated with taxes.

In this case, the utility function of supply (U) can be expressed through the following formulation:

$$U_o = \bar{P} - \left(P_{MinO} + \frac{c}{r*} \right)$$

Where:
U = the utility function of supply;
P segnato = the equilibrium price;
P_m = the minimum price required by the bidder;
C = costs linked to conservation;
$r*$ = the discount rate; and
$c/r*$ = the capitalised costs.

Accordingly, from the supply side, the benefit derived from the sale, in financial terms, is proportional to the sale price (considered after tax, which, for simplicity, is not considered in this analysis) minus the minimum price that the bidder is willing to accept, increased by the discounted cost of conserving the asset. At this point, it is possible to identify the equilibrium price (P segnato), which, in the model described, is identified as a value within the set of numbers bounded by the utility function of demand and the utility function of supply. The below equation can be solved to arrive at a specific value for P segnato:

$$U_o = U_d \rightarrow \frac{\overline{P} - \left(P_{MinO} + \dfrac{c}{r*} \right)}{r_o} = \frac{P_{MaxD} - \overline{P}}{r_d}$$

$$\overline{P} = \frac{r_o * P_{MaxD} + \dfrac{r_d * c}{r*} + rd * P_{MinO}}{r_o + r_d}$$

Where:

P segnato = the equilibrium price (i.e. the unknown);

r_o = the discount rate, referring to the supply (i.e. the bidder's opportunity cost, corresponding to his or her lack of future returns resulting from the asset's sale);

P_{MaxD} = the maximum price that the asker is willing to pay;

r_d = the discount rate for the demand, equivalent to the demand's opportunity cost (i.e. the minimum yield expected from the investment);

C = the costs of conserving, maintaining and developing the asset;

r' = the discounted rate, which differs from r_o and r_d because it refers to a wider project horizon and is comparable to a risk-free discount rate;

P_{MinD} = the minimum price required by the bidder.

Economic approach

It is also possible to estimate the value of a heritage asset by measuring the consumptive and prospective economic value that is made or destroyed by the public or private entity that manages the asset.

In order to arrive at an accurate quantification of created value, it is necessary to associate an operating income measure (e.g. net operating profit after taxes; NOPAT) with the cost capital employed.

The indicator that best pursues this aim is economic value added (EVA)[9] which measures the efficiency with which a company uses its invested capital and, accordingly, the company's capacity to create economic value by managing that capital. It can be expressed in the following equation:

$$EVR^R = Nopat - (Capitale\,impiegato*Wacc)$$

Where:
NOPAT = business operating income, less taxes;
invested capital (CI) = the sum of net worth and reserve funds; and
WAAC = the weighted average cost of capital.

WAAC, which expresses the company's weighted cost of capital and the relative cost of any borrowed and venture capital, can be calculated using the following formula:

$$Wacc = (D*K_d + E*K_e)/D + E$$

Where:
E = net worth, increased by reserve funds (where applicable);
D = total liabilities;
K_e = the cost of equity capital (discussed further below); and
K_d = the cost of equity capital taken on credit, calculated as a percentage of the amount of interest paid on liabilities during the reference period to the total liabilities in the same period.

Using the methodology known as the capital asset pricing model (CAPM), Ke can be determined with the following formula:

$$K_e = r_f + \beta(r_m - r_f)$$

Where:
r_f = the rate of risk-free yield, estimated as the average yield of a top-rated 10-year government bond;
r_m = the expected market return for a similar investment;
β = the beta of the bond, expressing historical changes in the share price of the managing company (measuring the sensitivity of the share price to changes in the market index; If the company is unlisted, the beta is calculated using comparables).

To determine EVA^R (EVA for the reference period), it is necessary to broaden the analysis of potential income to cover a medium- to long-term time horizon. For this, it is appropriate to associate this static measure of value created to a metric of the economic value of the company that manages the asset.

This latter value can be estimated as the sum of two components:

- the current operation value (COV), represented by the sum of the CI and the current EVA (EVA$_c$), discounted for WAAC; this value is similar to the company's discounted value, linked to the profitability and economic value created at the measurement date; and
- the future growth value (FGV), which represents the current value of the increase expected in the EVA$_c$ (assumed constant); this value is equivalent to the 'G' rate in the projection horizon, and is assumed to be infinite and to reflect all future growth opportunities in the market.

Accordingly, measurement of the value of a heritage asset through the consumptive and prospective economic value that is created or destroyed by the public or private body that manages the asset can be achieved using the following formula:

$$V_{HA} = COV + FGV =$$
$$= [C.I. + (EVA_c / Wacc) + [(EVA_c) / (Wacc - g)]$$

Whenever the individual variables of formula are those described previous in paragraph and are worth the assumption of estimation of company's economic value in a infinitive time horizon, so how a perpetual annuity, other the assumptions that EVA's current percentage rate of future increase, estimated constant and equal to 'g' rate, is less than WAAC.

Financial approach

This section presents a method for estimating a heritage asset's value using purely financial measures – namely the discounted cash flows of the company that manages the asset (i.e. the asset's touristic or usage value) and the discounted cash flow of the public or private investments that support the asset's protection, conservation or exploitation (i.e. the asset's intrinsic value)[10].

The heritage asset value (V_{HA}) is therefore equal to the sum of its touristic or usage value (VT_{HA}) and its intrinsic value (VI_{HA}):

$$V_{HA} = VT_{HA} + VI_{HA}$$

VTH$_{HA}$ is estimated using the following formula:

$$VT_{HA} = \sum_{t=1}^{n} \frac{FC_t + FCI_t - CGD_t}{(1+i)^t}$$

Where:

FC_t = the immediate cash flows generated by the public or private body that manages the heritage asset (typically revenues from entrance or concession fees) at time 't', summed over the projection horizon;

FCI_t = the indirect cash flows generated by the heritage asset for the regional economy (via tourists) at time t, summed over the project horizon;

CGD_t = the direct costs of managing the asset (e.g. costs relating to staff, raw materials, consumables, consumer goods, services and third-party goods) at time 't', summed over the project horizon; and

I = the discount rate, which reflects the level of risk estimated in the cash flows and, accordingly, the managing company's level of risk; this discount rate may also be estimated as an opportunity cost and subsequently imposed as a required ROI for investments characterised by similar risk profiles.

In contrast, the VI_{HA} of a heritage asset is determined as a summation of all public or private investments for the asset's protection, conservation or exploitation over the same projection horizon as that utilised for the estimate of VT_{HA}, but it does not include operating revenues that are re-invested by the managing company for this purpose. In other words, the VI_{HA} considers only the financial resources provided by non-managing entities (i.e. public and private bodies, citizens) for the protection, conservation or exploitation of the asset and excludes any investments in the asset from the entity that manages it. The resulting estimates of financial flows are discounted at the same rate as that used to estimate VT_{HA}.

The estimation of cash flows used to determine both VT_{HA} and VI_{HA} refer to time 't'; this may represent cash flows produced in the previous year of management or an average of flows generated over the prior three or five years. The discount rate 'i' is a perpetual revenue, assuming continuity in the asset's economic viability.

Medium value method

The final method used to estimate the value of heritage assets discussed here draws on the professional judgement of a group of independent and anonymous experts, building on the so-called 'Delphi method'.[11] The Delphi method is an iterative survey measure that determines, following multiple stages of expression and evaluation, the opinions of a group of independent and anonymous experts. In this process, a coordinator known as a 'facilitator' determines the most comprehensive and widespread opinion or, as in the present case, value that emerges from the expert feedback.

The facilitator sends a questionnaire (or a single question) to a select group of experts whose identity remains anonymous to others in the group. The experts give their opinion on the question(s), and they may subsequently be re-solicited by the facilitator to elaborate on their responses, until the process concludes.

Applied to the valuation of heritage assets, the method seems useful and complementary to the previously explored methodologies, because of the complexity involved in evaluating the economic and patrimonial value of these unique assets. The method enables the judgement of a group of experts (selected on account of their specific skills) to be synthesised, while maintaining the experts' anonymity in order to reduce the risk of bias caused by undue interactions between them and the external context.

With regard to the valuation of heritage assets, in this process, the expert participants express their assessment of the economic and/or patrimonial value of a specific heritage asset. The facilitator may request further elaboration from particular experts, either through follow-up questions or requests for clarification. Such requests for clarification may also refer to judgements expressed by other experts in the group, which again, are shared under the veil of anonymity. Following multiple iterations of this process, the facilitator proceeds to synthesise the final judgement of the expert group into a single – reasoned and well-informed – answer. In order to determine this synthesis value, it is suggested that the facilitator remove the highest and lowest values set out by the expert group and take an arithmetic mean of the remaining values.

Notes

1 The authors hold that the preservation/conservation of a cultural or landscape asset is not separate from the exploitation of that asset but should instead be considered integral to enhancing the asset's economic value. The fundamental principle of exploitation was first introduced by the Codice dei beni culturali e del paesaggio (DL No. 42 of 22 January 2004) as a necessary protective action. In economic terms, enhancement means increasing the value of an asset (i.e. making its value explicit, not expressed; in the case of a heritage asset, under conditions of physical degradation). The exploitation of a particular cultural or landscape good can be evaluated using a set of direct measures (e.g. physical recovery, such as a renovation; or a conservative intervention, such as re-functioning) and, simultaneously, in interventions involving the surrounding antrophic or natural area, depending on whether the good is placed in an urban context. For greater insight on these points, reference is made, *inter alia*, to Manganelli (2007).

2 In a company assessment process, it is typical to start with net worth, which is equivalent to the difference between the company's budgeted activities and passivities. However, as accounting policies are often firm-specific, net worth does not necessarily always provide an exact estimate of the company's value. On this theme, reference is made, *inter alia*, to Onida (1963, pp. 715–716); Amaduzzi (1978, p. 106); Giovannini (1999a, p. 308); and Giovannini (1999b, p. 2). This section was freely inspired by – but properly contextualised within – Pacelli's (2007) case of a company that managing heritage assets.

3 For a deeper analysis of the efficiency of financial markets, see, *inter alia*, Fama (1970); Grossman (1976); Grossman and Stiglitz (1980); Campbell and Kracaw (1980); Stiglitz and Weiss (1981); Millon and Thakor (1985); Chan and Thakor (1987); and Allen (1990).

4 Needless to point out, in professional practice, a myriad of valuation methods are used, of which most are classifiable in one of the methodological families listed here. As the purpose of this section is not to present a deep analysis of the classification of valuation methods, the taxonomy produced must not be considered exhaustive, just as the description of the methods does not presume to be complete and detailed. For deeper insight into the valuation of companies, reference is made, *inter alia*, to Berti (2009); Damodaran (2010); and Damodaran and Roggi (2011).

5 For a deeper discussion of valuing intangibles, reference is made, *inter alia*, to Pacelli (2007).

6 If the income correction is positive, it assumes the name 'goodwill'; otherwise, if it is negative, it is called 'badwill'.

7 For a wider examination of the methods used to value heritage assets, reference is made, *inter alia*, to: Del Sordo and Levy Orelli (2012); Aa. Vv. (2014); Aversano (2015); Biondi (2018).

8 The model presented in this sub-section borrows liberally from Manganelli (2007), to whom reference is made for further consideration.

9 For insights into the EVA methodology, reference is made, *inter alia*, to Aiaf (1998); Natale and Sarrocco (2001); Dell'Atti and Pacelli (2006); Pacelli (2007).

10 The model presented in this section was freely inspired D'Angeli et al. (2018) yet substantially reviewed and revised.

11 For more details on the Delphi method, reference is made, *inter alia*, to: Abd Manaf (2008); Lee and King (2008); Saunders et al. (2009); Geist (2010); Worrell, Di Gangi and Bush (2013); Vollero and Palazzo (2015); Strand, Carson, Navrud, Ortiz-Bobea and Vincent (2017).

References

AA., VV. (2014), *I valori del museo: Strumenti e prospettive manageriali*, Franco Angeli, Milano.

Abd Manaf, Z. (2008), "Establishing the national digital cultural heritage repository in Malaysia", in *Library Review – Emerald*, n. 57/2008.

Aiaf (1998), "L'Economic Value Added (EVA): Principi teorici", in *Quaderno di ricerca n. 90.*

Allen, F. (1990), "The market for information and the origin of financial intermediation", in *Journal of Financial Intermediation*, Vol.1.

Amaduzzi, A. (1978), *L'azienda*, Utet, Torino.

Aversano, N. (2015), *La contabilizzazione degli heritage assets negli enti locali: Esperienze internazionali a confronto*, Giappichelli, Torino.

Biondi, L. (2018), *La valutazione del patrimonio culturale nel bilancio delle pubbliche amministrazioni: Accounting for heritage assets*, CEDAM, Padova.

Berti, A. (2009), *La qualità degli affidamenti: La valutazione del rischio di credito nel rapporto banca-impresa*, Franco Angeli, Milano.

Campbell, T., Kracaw W. (1980), "Information production, market signalling and the theory of financial intermediation", in *Journal of Finance*, n. 35.

Chan, Y., Thakor, A.V. (1987), "Collateral and competitive equilibria with moral hazard and private information", in *Journal of Finance*, n. 42.

Damodaran, A., Roggi, O. (2011), *Finanza aziendale*, Apogeo, Milano.

Damodaran, A. (2010), *Valutazione delle aziende*, Apogeo, Milano.

D'Angeli, P., Martino, G., Maurizi, S., Minuti, M. (2018), "Valutare il patrimonio culturale nella prospettiva internazionale: Una proposta di metodo", in *Il Giornale delle Fondazioni*, 29 aprile 2018.

Dell'Atti, S., Pacelli, V. (2006), "Prezzo e valore nelle banche: Un'analisi empirica nei principali gruppi bancari italiani", in *Banche e Banchieri*, n. 6.

Del Sordo C., Levy Orelli R. (2012), *Profili economico-aziendali e di bilancio delle organizzazioni culturali*, Franco Angeli, Milano.

Fama, E.F. (1970), "Efficient capital market: A review of theory and empirical work", in *Journal of Finance*, May.

Geist, M.R. (2010), "Using the Delphi method to engage stakeholders: A comparison of two studies", in *Evaluation and Program Planning – Elsevier*, n. 33/2010.

Giovannini, P. (1999a), "Variazioni di capitale economico e stima del corso azionario di equilibrio", in *Banche e Banchieri*, n. 4.

Giovannini, P. (1999b), *Capitale economico e capitale netto nella formazione del corso azionario*, Quaderni della Scuola Superiore di Tecnica Aziendale, Edizioni Kappa, Roma.

Grossman, S.J. (1976), "On the efficiency of competitive stock markets where traders have different information", in *Journal of Finance*, Vol. XXXI, n.2, May.

Grossman, S.J., Stiglitz, J.E. (1980), "On the impossibility of informatively efficient markets", in *American Economic Review*, Vol. 70, June.

Guatri L., Bini M. (2005), *Nuovo trattato sulla valutazione delle aziende*, Università Bocconi Editore, Milano;

Lee, C.F., King, B.E. (2008), "Using the Delphi method to assess the potential of Taiwan's hot springs tourism sector", in *International Journal of Tourism Research – John Wiley & Sons*, n. 10/2008.

Manganelli, B. (2007), "Valutazioni economico-estimative nella valorizzazione di edifici storico-architettonici", in *Aestimum*, n. 51, pp. 21–42.

Millon, M., Thakor, A.V. (1985), "Moral Hazard and information sharing: A model of financial information gathering agencies", in *Journal of Finance*, n. 40, December.

Natale, E., Sarrocco, F. (2001), *Il value based management nelle banche: La nuova banca orientata al valore: modelli teorici e applicazioni pratiche*, Il Sole 24Ore, Milano.

Onida, P. (1963), *Economia aziendale*, Utet, Torino.

Pacelli, V. (2007), *Capitale, rischio e valore nelle banche*, Edizioni Scientifiche Italiane, Napoli.

Saunders, M., Lewis, P., Thornhill, A. (2009), *Research methods for business students*, Harlow, Pearson Education Limited.

Strand, J., Carson, R.T., Navrud, S., Ortiz-Bobea, A., Vincent, J.R. (2017), "Using the Delphi method to value protection of the Amazon rainforest", in *Ecological Economics – Elsevier*, n. 131/2017.

Stiglitz, J.E., Weiss, A. (1981), "Credit rationing in markets with imperfect information", in *American Economic Review*, n. 71.

Vollero, A., Palazzo, M. (2015), "Conceptualizing content marketing: a delphi approach", in *Mercati e Competitività – Franco Angeli*, n. 1/2015.

Worrell, J.L., Di Gangi, P.M., Bush, A.A. (2013), "Exploring the use of the Delphi method in accounting information systems research", in *International Journal of Accounting Information System – Elsevier*, n. 14/2013.

5 Caves as environmental and tourist resources

Analysis of the Waitomo Glowworm Caves and the Caves of Castellana

Introduction

Speleological tourism (i.e. tourism linked to caves), is a valuable economic resource for many global regions. This is particularly true for Italy, which boasts a large number of natural cavities equipped for tourism. It is estimated that, today, Italian tourist caves register more than 1.5 million visitors each year, generating an aggregate annual turnover of approximately 20 million euros. This figure significantly expands when one takes into account collateral services to cave visits, such as speleological museums and nearby vendors. Furthermore, the annual turnover may double when allied industries or services provided by third parties, such as catering, accommodation and commercial and sports activities, are considered. Thus, from an aptly enhanced tourist cave, a number of collateral activities may arise in the service and hospitality fields; such activities not only provide employment opportunities, but they also attract public and private investments and therefore feed a virtuous cycle with multiplier effects on production and regional income.

This chapter analyses caves as an environmental and tourist resource, first describing the state of play of Italian caves and then exploring the cases of the Waitomo Glowworm Caves in New Zealand and the Castellana Caves in Italy.

Italian caves as an environmental and tourist resource

According to data provided by Francescantonio D'Orilia, President of the Association of Italian Tourist Caves (AGTI), the MIdA Foundation and the Pertosa-Auletta Caves[1] register more than 1.5 million visitors each year, generating an aggregate annual turnover of approximately 20 million euros. This figure significantly expands when one takes into account collateral services to cave visits, such as speleological museums and nearby vendors. Furthermore, the annual turnover may double when allied industries or services provided by third parties, such as catering, accommodation and commercial and sports activities, are considered. Speleological tourism is therefore a precious economic resource in Italy, which boasts a large number of natural cavities equipped for tourism, providing a safe and accessible visitor experience. Italian tourist caves are typically associated with karst landscapes, which are present in specific regions of the country. These landscapes, which are formed via dissolution, are characterised by rocky outcrops (generally limestone), sinkholes, blind valleys and caves. Furthermore, the flow of slightly acidic meteoric waters to the subsoil produces an epigeous and hypogeal morphology characterised by numerous discontinuities and fractures. Such rock formations, which vary widely in form, are found in approximately one-quarter of the Italian territory.

In Emilia-Romagna, for example, karst landscapes constitute less than 1% of the regional area, while in Umbria they cover more than 50%. Areas of particular importance include the Karst of Trieste, the Dolomites, the Maiella, the Matese and the Murge. However, the number and size of the caves in these landscapes is not proportional to the geographic extent of their area, but depends on the type of rock, the tectonics and the intensity of rainfall in the area, either currently or historically. The Italian region with the most tourist caves – of which some are of particular geological and tourist importance – is Sardinia, where karst landscapes represent only a very limited percentage of the overall region (9%). Karst regions that are greater in size – with some almost as big as Sardinia, itself – can be found in Marche, Umbria, Lazio and Abruzzo; however, in these areas, there are only six tourist caves. Puglia, which is almost 50% karst, has only five tourist caves, of which only one is of large dimensions (Grotte di Castellana) (Verole-Bozzello, 2014).

According to the updated census from the Association of Italian Tourist Grottos (AGTI), there are currently 48 tourist caves and 42 semi-tourist caves in Italy,[2] with the highest concentration in Sardinia (12 tourist and 4 semi-tourist caves). The only regions without tourist caves are Trentino-Alto Adige, Valle d'Aosta, Emilia-Romagna, Umbria, Molise and Sicily.

Among these natural cavities, some are very small in size (in the order of a few tens of meters), and rarely require more than 15 minutes to visit. Others are characterised by a compound development and require up to three hours to visit. Even the number of annual visitors is extremely variable, with some caves recording fewer than a thousand visitors per year and others receiving more than 300,000. The most visited Italian caves are those of Frasassi in the Marches and Castellana Grotte in Puglia, which, in addition to being particularly fascinating environmental features (due to their geographical location) and tourist attractions, are probably also the best served by public transport (Verole-Bozzello, 2014). A later section of this chapter is dedicated to a detailed analysis of the Caves of Castellana. However, the Frasassi Caves are also an important tourist cave complex with more than 13 km of tunnels and paths. These caves offer one of the most grandiose and evocative underground routes in the world. For instance, one of its interior features is the Abyss Ancona – a gigantic underground cavity (among the largest in the world) measuring 180 m long, 120 m wide and 200 m high – large enough to contain Milan Cathedral.

Other tourist caves, featuring well-organised and safe walking paths and enjoying a recognised tradition for tourism include: the Cave of Bossea in Fabrosa Soprana (Piedmont), which has been open to the public since 1874; the Toirano Caves (Liguria), which comprise more than 150 natural caves; the Caves of Neptune in Alghero (Sardinia), which were discovered in the 18th century within the protected marine area of Capo Caccia; the Giant Cave in Sgonico (Friuli Venezia Giulia), which is the largest tourist cavity in the world, formed by a single hall of more than 98 m high that is reached via an imposing staircase of 360 stone steps; the Pastena Caves (Lazio), which were discovered in 1926 and include ten rooms of stalactites and stalagmites, ponds and waterfalls; and the Pertosa-Auletta Caves in Campania, which are the only non-marine caves in Italy that are crossed by a river (i.e. the Negro River).

In Italy, tourist caves are often located in geographical areas that are poor in resources or underdeveloped; therefore, when properly valued and managed, they can develop into a lifeboat (first) and flywheel (second) for the regional economy, whereas they might otherwise be destined for degradation. An appropriately enhanced tourist cave – attracting tens or hundreds of thousands of tourists each year – may give rise to various collateral activities, in terms of both services and hospitality. In this way, it may provide numerous employment opportunities and attract public or private investment, thereby feeding a virtuous cycle with multiplier effects on regional production and income. Regional investment is particularly important for the development of infrastructure and services to improve the accessibility of tourist attractions and make the visitor experience more pleasant. This is likely to increase the number of tourists, benefiting both the entire regional economy and the entity that manages the attraction.

In other words, it is necessary to prevent a tourist cave from remaining a 'cathedral in the desert' by investing in the infrastructure and facilities/services that surround it. Such support structures may include accommodation facilities, restaurants, theme parks, museums, scientific and educational laboratories (open to tourists), amphitheatres, secondary tourist attractions, bookshops, local food and handicraft vendors, natural landscape attractions, sports facilities and entertainment venues. None of these entities should distort or contaminate the natural environment in which the cave is located, but each should enhance it harmoniously in order to improve the visitor experience. Therefore, professionalism and technical and managerial training are needed, as well as entrepreneurial spirit and investment, to mine value from these natural resources. In contrast, improvisation and arrogance risk damaging the image, reputation and economic value of the tourist attraction and its region.

For this reason, speleological training for cave guides and managerial training for cave administrators is important, although not universally practiced. It should therefore be a priority for cave administrators to invest in their own training as managers of a complex environmental asset as well as the training of their personnel, so that management of the asset is made efficient and profitable and the visitor experience is improved; this should benefit not only the managing body directly, but also the entire system of Italian tourist caves. In this sense, as also highlighted by D'Orilia, a priority objective of AGTI is to organise training courses for operators and managers of the associated caves. Other relevant aspects and priorities for AGTI, although logically conflicting, are those of environmental sustainability, promotion and marketing. Environmental sustainability should be preserved through continuous scientific surveys and appropriate protective interventions to reverse the exposure of caves to harmful external elements brought about by mass tourism.

The promotion and marketing of Italian tourist caves, on the other hand, should be modernised using techniques (e.g. digital techniques) that are already common in other sectors. Marketing campaigns should promote not only individual caves, but also the local tourism system and entire complex of Italian tourist caves. It is therefore necessary to create a network of Italian caves, both logistically and commercially, and to promote the caves in this network alongside nearby tourist attractions in order to offer visitors an integrated tourist offer and thereby create regional value.

Waitomo Glowworm Caves

The Waitomo Glowworm Caves, located on the edge of the Waitomo Caves in King Country, New Zealand, has been a major tourist attraction for almost 130 years. Formed approximately 30 million years ago, the caves are populated by luminescent insects (glowworms) that, in the dark, light up in green or blue (similar to fireflies), creating the effect of a starry sky on the vaults of the cave. In addition to the Waitomo Glowworm Cave, the Waitomo compound includes two other caves (Aranui and Ruakuri). In December 1887, British Inspector Fred Mace and Chief Maori Taane Tinorou were the first people to explore the point where an underground river entered what was called by the Maori, *waitomo* ('water entering a hole in the ground'). In 1889, the Department of the Crown Lands led the first mapping expedition and first photographic surveys of the caves, and, more or less in the same period, the first commercial tours of what is now known as the Glowworm Caves were conducted by Tinorou. In the 19 months between June 1889 and December 1890, 360 visitors toured and admired the compound.

With the Scenery Preservation Act of 1903, the Waitomo Glowworm Caves became government property. They were subsequently put under the control of the Department of Tourism and became the most profitable of all publicly owned tourist settlements in New Zealand (Arrel 1984). In 1990, 75% of the property passed to the Maori, while the remaining 25% remained the property of the New Zealand government, under the Department of Conservation.

The Maori property is currently managed by the Ruapuha-Uekaha Hapu Trust – the government of which includes two families that descended from Taane Tinorou. Management of the caves, the Waitomo Caves Hotel and the Waitomo Tavern are subject to a 32-year lease between the property, the Ruapuha-Uekaha Hapu Trust, the New Zealand Department of Conservation and the Tourism Holdings Company Limited; these bodies took over the contract from the South Pacific Hotel Corporation (SPHC) in 1996.

In 2016, more than 500,000 people visited the caves, generating revenue of approximately 71 million Australian dollars (approximately 43 million euros). These figures make Waitomo the most visited speleological compound in the Southern hemisphere. The cost of a visitor's ticket to the Glowworm Cave is only 51 Australian dollars (approximately 31 euros), while the ticket to also visit the Aranui and Ruakuri caves is 97 dollars (approximately 60 euros). In addition, visitors may register for two tourist experiences: 'Black Abyss', a five-hour speleological course sold for 246 Australian dollars; and 'Black Labyrinth', three hours of rafting in the darkness of Ruakuri Cave, at the cost of 142 Australian dollars.

There is no reliable information on the number of national visitors to the Waitomo Caves, although data provided by the Waitomo Caves Hotel indicate that the New Zealand market makes up approximately 8% of its total visitors. Cave visits are seasonal: in the peak season of November through April, the cave receives up to 3,000 visitors a day, with most arriving between 11 am and 2 pm.

The number of visitors to the Waitomo compound has grown by 100,000 in the last ten years, thereby exacerbating the significant environmental impact of the caves. In particular, visitors to the cave not only generate waste inside and around the caves, but each visitor also emits 170W of energy, which can interfere (as in breath) with the natural humidity of the environment and impact the cave's internal ecosystem. Further, if the walls and concretions of the caves are touched, they deteriorate over time due to the natural substances present in human skin. Changes to the structure of the caves also reduces the number of glowworms present. Even the increased lighting of the caves, which is naturally dark, has a negative impact on its calcareous formations, which over time may develop a covering of a substance similar to *lampenflora* moss.

The increase in tourists over the last decade, as well as weighing on the internal environment of the caves, has also put pressure on the receptive capacities of the local village, as the Tourism Holdings Chief Operating Officer Jo Allison, who manages the caves, declared to the *New Zealand Herald*. In particular, the facilities dedicated to welcoming tourists are not sufficient, especially during peak periods. Recently, the managing body, in agreement with the municipal administration, created a new parking lot, doubled the commercial area for the sale of souvenirs and created a new bar-restaurant compound. Although the main concern of the cave operators remains the increase in carbon dioxide levels inside the caves, looking to the future, they also aim at increasing the accommodation capacity near the caves to ensure the sustainability of the increased tourist flow.

Castellana Caves

This section analyses the case of the Castellana Caves, starting with their geological and tourist genesis then describing their governance model, development strategies, management problems, financial performance and contribution to the tourism industry and local and regional economies, and closing with an eye to the future. In order to provide a detailed and wide picture, we analyse all of the company's financial statements, from its constitution to the present day, as well as the relevant bylaws – the Articles of Incorporation and agreements with the Municipality of Castellana Grotte. We also draw on data from a focus group held on 9 July 2018 and a questionnaire involving all Presidents of the Board of Directors of Grotte di Castellana who had held the position for at least 6 months, from the company's establishment to the present day (that is, in chronological order of mandate: Cosimo Cisternino, Giuseppe Savino, Maurizio Tommaso Pace, Domenico Ciliberti, Marica Pace and Victor Joal Casulli).[3]

Geological and tourist genesis of the Castellana Caves

The karst compound of the Castellana Caves was discovered on 23 January 1938 during the now famous descent of the speleologist Franco Anelli, from the Italian Institute of Speleology of Postumia, who was assigned by the Provincial Tourism Board of Bari to carry out a speleological survey in Puglia.[4] On 23 January 1938, Anelli reached the bottom of the cave's 'Grave' and immediately realised that he was facing a vast karstic compound of extreme scientific interest, as well as tourist value.[5]

Prior to that time, the natural entrance to the karst compound – the so-called 'Grave' or 'Devil's Hole' – was viewed with fear and superstition by the local population and used as a large landfill. Entrance to the Grave – the deep hole in the cave entrance – inspired a sense of anguish and fear in those who travelled the nearby country road, especially at dusk, when one could see the exit of bats and vapours from the abyss. These were superstitiously considered the wandering souls of suicides, trying in vain to reach heaven. Although it is legitimate to attribute to Anelli the scientific discovery of the Castellana Caves in 1938, it is not possible to say with certainty that Anelli was the first man to venture into the Grave, as it is likely that other daring persons had previously explored it, though certainly with less scientific awareness and fewer technical resources.

According to some legends, Vincenzo Longo (1737–1825), a humanist and juris consult of Castellana Grotte, was the first man to descend into the Grave, together with a large group of youth around his own age. Memories of this expedition, enriched by various details, were perpetuated by witnesses and conveyed to later generations, to the extent that, in the nineteenth century, the chorographic-universal *Dictionary of Italy* attested to the historicity of the event:

> A little more than a mile to the west of Castellana I had a natural curiosity, that is a sinkhole called by the vulgar the 'Grave'; the mouth of this has a circumference of about 180 palms and the depth is about 300 palms. In the last century some intrepid citizens of Castellana descended early morning, using hawsers and ropes, and walked down more miles of dark underground districts, and they did not come out until around midnight, so that the relatives and friends fluttered for a long wait.

When, in the winter of 1938, Anelli made his own descent into the dark Grave, he was likely driven by curiosity yet aware of the trepidation of the local population, and probably also felt the same conflicting feelings of disquiet and hope that animate all those who venture into the unknown. The historic date of 23 January 1938 remains the starting point of the adventure of the Castellana Caves as a scientific, tourist and economic phenomenon, and it also marks a turning point in the history for the City of Castellana, which was later renamed (in 1950) Castellana Grotte in tribute to its karst compound. Beginning in the 1960s, the larger region, which had previously been based on a rural economy, saw a revival in tourism and economic growth due to the flow of visitors wishing to venture into its caves.

Today, the Castellana Caves are the most visited payed tourist attraction in Puglia, and among the top 20 attractions in Italy, which otherwise enjoys more than 8,000 paid tourist attractions, as well as a priceless natural heritage. Located in the heart of the Valle d'Itria in Puglia, 40 km southeast of the regional capital of Bari, 60 km from the stones of Matera, 15 km from the Trulli of Alberobello and the beautiful seas of Monopoli and Polignano a Mare and a few kilometres from urban areas (e.g. Conversano, Putignano, Fasano, Locorotondo), the Castellana Caves are situated in an evocative territory offering a wide and diversified set of tourism opportunities. Each year, the caves attract hundreds of thousands of visitors from across the world, and, since their discovery to the present day, they have accommodated more than 17 million. This impressive tourist flow has generated, over the caves' 80-year history, a volume of direct business (i.e. revenues earned directly from cave visits) of more 80 million euros, of which almost 65% has been generated in the past 18 years (since the establishment of Grotte di Castellana) and the remaining 35% generated in the prior 61 years.

Geologically, the hypogeum compound is contained in a rock mass that is thought to have originated more than 85 million years ago; the caves, themselves, have been dated back approximately 2 million years. The caves are located on the calcareous plateau of the southeastern Murge, formed in the Upper Cretaceous epoch. The Castellana region is characterised by limestone rocks composed essentially of calcium carbonate. In particular, the limestone in this area is called Altamura limestone. The Castellana Caves are 3.348 m in length and reach a maximum depth of 122 m from the surface. The temperature of the interior rooms is approximately 18°C. The entire region of the Castellana Caves features elements that geology links to the development of all phenomenologies of karst. Specifically, the superficial landscape is characterised by the presence of a wide spread of blades, sinkholes and swallow holes that model the morphology to a unique work of art.

The most spectacular articulations of the underground karst system of the Castellana Caves are represented by the majestic Grave (a natural pantheon that is 100 m long, 50 m wide and 60 m deep, and the only cavity of the compound with direct access to the outside) and the splendid White Cave (approximately 1.2 km from the entrance, at a depth of 75 m). The most fascinating aspect of the caves' aesthetic landscape is their concretion – that is, the limestone deposits that cover the bare walls that, over many years, have been brought into suspension by the slow crossing of rainwater over the overlying rocky layers; once the rainwater reaches the empty space of the caves, it drips to the vault and the floor, leaving a calcium carbonate deposit that develops into stalactites (on the vault) and stalagmites (on the floor).

The descending staircase of the entrance tunnel, which was dug by Sardinian miners following Anelli's initial descent, offers visitors a prime vantage point from which to directly observe the caves' rocky layers. These layers were formed by the accumulation and superposition of carbonate sludge in the shallow sea cretaceous environment. Subsequently, the mud – once lithified – formed into layered packs of rock that are still visible. The lower rocky layer, which was formed first, is older than the upper layer. When visitors descend the steps of the tunnel leading into the caves, they can therefore imagine going back in geological time.

Grotte di Castellana: Corporate purpose, social object and governance

Grotte di Castellana was created through Articles of Association dated 8 April 1999 from the notary Corrado Magarelli, which bears the signature of Simone Cosimo Leone Pinto (i.e. the Pro Tempore Mayor of Castellana Grotte). Pinto, the sole member of the constituting company, later appointed Cosimo Cisternino as the first Pro Tempore President of the company's Board of Directors. Article 3 of the Articles of Association, which defines the corporate purpose of Grotte di Castellana, establishes economic and environmental protection objectives that transcend national borders and managerial/operational criteria inspired by the concepts of efficiency, productivity, economy and speed (including operational speed). In particular, it outlines the following corporate objectives:

- to autonomously manage the Castellana Caves, extending care, protection and conservation, while also working to preserve and improve the image of the larger region by protecting its environment, supporting its tourist assets and encouraging its social, cultural and speleological development;

- to operate in partnership with the Municipality of Castellana Grotte, with respect to both the Castellana Caves and the Municipal Demanio;
- to promote scientific studies and initiatives towards conservation and protection (understood in terms of ecological defence and environmental pollution, as well as human impact) to improve and explore the use and development of the geological heritage;
- to direct, safeguard and manage the promotion of economic, craft, cultural, publishing, sporting and social initiatives and activities related to the compound and its operations, and to promote the Castellana Caves through live shows and theatrical and cinematographic events;
- to manage commercial aspects of the tourist activity, including the sale of goods and the supply of food and beverages;
- to perform ordinary and extraordinary maintenance of the goods and services relating to the compound;
- to strengthen and implement support structures for productive tourism, either directly or via third parties, including infrastructure and services relevant to the growth of the brand and the productivity of the compound;
- to respect state, regional and community laws (already in force or transposing) when studying, implementing, constructing or managing plants and infrastructures that are either related to or necessary for the best functioning, productivity and brand management of the compound;
- to promote and disseminate, also for advertising purposes, the interest and brand of the 'Bene Ambientale Grotte' in order to enhance its touristic potential;
- to seek and mobilise resources from any party, including international parties, for the financing of plans, programmes and projects regarding to the complex;
- to participate in programmes, projects and initiatives led by other companies, consortia and local authorities that share the 'Bene Ambientale Grotte' affiliation, either domestically or internationally;
- to promote and support the production, marketing and export of handcrafted products and related municipal and regional services connected with the compound; and
- to engage the services of travel agencies to organise, promote and implement the sale of tourist trips (including air, sea and land trips), for both Italian and foreign tourists.

As intended in the Articles of Association, on 7 December 1999, the Municipality of Castellana Grotte granted a deed for the compound including the Castellana Caves to the Chairman of Grotte di Castellana, Cosimo Cisternino. This initial ten-year convention was valid from 1 January 2000, and it was renewed twice on the dates of 17 December 2009 and 24 April 2017, respectively; it is next due to expire on 31 December 2019. According to the deed, the managing company undertakes to pay the Municipality of Castellana Grotte an annual fee, payable via deferred quarterly payments, amounting to 30.19% of the takings from the sale of visitor tickets to the caves, with a minimum guaranteed annual payment of 671,393.97 euros. As will be better ascertained in the later analysis of the company's economic and financial data, after the first 8 years of management (2000–2007), the annual payment to the municipality significantly exceeded the minimum threshold, due to a gradual increase in visitors; in particular, a significant growth trend was evident in the period 2013–2017. It is necessary that point out that, in addition to paying an annual fee to the municipality, Grotte di Castellana – having generated revenue of more than 15 million euros – also makes financial contributions to local events organised by the town council or local bodies and associations. In this way, it represents a precious and generous source of financial resources for the community.[6]

Italian caves within the AGTI network are managed by a wide variety of governing bodies, including associations, consortia, town councils, limited liability companies with a single member belonging to the local municipality, cooperatives, private investors, speleological groups and foundations. As D'Orilia highlighted in his interview, the best economic performance generally stems from private or otherwise corporate management. However, in management structures linked to a municipal administration (and therefore public governance), the natural political influence on appointments and management strategies may make interrupt management and slow development. As mentioned, since 1999, the Castellana Caves have been managed by a limited liability company with a single member in the Municipality of Castellana Grotte; this person – the city's Pro Tempore Mayor – has the statutory task of naming the company president and board of directors every three years.

At a first – superficial – analysis, we might imagine that when a company is governed by a municipality – even in part, via a single member – the municipality will guarantee protection and administrative stability. In actual fact, however, this proprietary structure and governance model generates extreme administrative instability, limits managerial independence and constrains the actions of directors to the short term, only. This is because the board of directors is subject to renewal every three years, in line with local political cycles, and this inevitably influences the appointments. A further effect of this system is that it slows the development of infrastructural investment policies, which require several years to bear fruit, with obvious implications for management performance and economic and financial results. Unfortunately, this model of governance does not favour the appointment of the best candidates for administrative and managerial positions, since the logic of political partition may prevail over meritocratic criteria; indeed, this is a common challenge faced by public companies.

Finally, in terms of ownership structure and governance, although the present work does not pursue the aim of exploring legal and regulatory aspects in depth (despite acknowledging their relevance to corporate management), we cannot fail to point out the serious and concrete risk that a rigid, and in some ways short-sighted, interpretation and application of the legislation on in-house[7] companies may compromise the autonomy of the managing company and limit its operating margins. Over time, such a compromise will inevitably lead to a reduction in business volume and the bankruptcy of the funded company.

Development strategies

In the initial eight years of commercial activity (2000–2007), Grotte di Castellana was less oriented to tourism and commercial development and more oriented to environmental protection and speleological research. The first promotion of the caves, which elaborated on its hypogeum features, was presented online, through the launch of the Castellana Caves website. In 2008, however, Grotte di Castellana changed its marketing strategy, focusing more on tourist promotion, which it implemented via widespread participation in national and international fairs, collaboration with the Puglia Region (PugliaPromozione, Apulia Film Commission) and other localities, and opening the caves to artistic and cultural events targeting different market sectors. In the period 2008–2011, the company launched the 'Hell in the Cave' production, 'Speleonight' night visits and the 'Horror Caves' film festival. From 2008 onwards, the company continued this strategy of promoting tourism and trade with increased conviction, participating in national and international tourism fairs and organising cultural and artistic events to promote the cave brand, while also diversifying the visitor offer. This strategic breakthrough led to a period of stable economic growth that gradually consolidated the company's patrimonial solidity.

In particular, starting from 2013, the company entered a five-year period of significant and constant growth, leading it to achieve the greatest turnover in its history in the last accounting period. This period of constant growth was the result of the marked commercial orientation of the corporate strategy, which resulted in restyled communication, a better online presence and new logo, as well as the creation of the 'Meraviglia di Puglia' payoff, the 'Grotte Experience', new artistic and cultural events held inside the Grave, the 'Hell in the Cave' production, 'Speleonight' and 'Sirio' events, and the 'Episodi' programme of author talks – in collaboration with the Festival of the Libro Possibile – which hosted authors of international prestige. These developments, which were encouraged in large part by artists who periodically performed inside the caves, increased the visibility of the underground compound in the national media and enabled visitors to the Castellana Caves to take advantage of additional products beyond the natural experience of the caves, themselves. Moreover, during this period, commercial partnerships were forged with regional tourist attractions, carriers and accommodation facilities, producing satisfactory results.

Management criticalities

The previous section outlined the commercial and tourist strategies that have determined the significant growth of visitors to the Castellana Caves in recent years. This section, in contrast, highlights the management problems that have not yet been resolved.

First and foremost, it is necessary to highlight the logistical problems and consequent need for environmental, urban and architectural redevelopment of the area surrounding the karst compound. These criticalities inhibit the development of commercial and tourist activities related to visiting the caves and, at the same time, are aesthetically displeasing to visitors. Substantial public and private investment is needed to connect the karst compound to the city centre and to other regional attractions. Similarly, environmental, urban and architectural redevelopment is needed to create an ideal environment for the development of collateral business activities, with respect to services, entertainment and accommodation; such activities would not only provide new employment opportunities, but would also attract public and private investment and thereby feed a virtuous cycle generating multiplier effects for regional production and income. Such investments could be obtained from private and public entities, as well as the managing company (through investment of free capital reserves, in support of valorisation). Irrespective of its source, investment in infrastructure and services is needed to facilitate tourism and enhance the visitor experience, while also reducing the localisation and seasonality of the tourist flow and increasing tourists' average time spent in the region; all of these effects would have a profoundly positive impact on the regional entire economy. The organisation of events or the creation of secondary tourist attractions near the caves – even outside the immediate area of Castellana – would be likely to attract visitors in the off-season, thus reducing the seasonality of tourist flows; this would not only facilitate the diversification of revenue sources, but it would also contribute to protecting the environmental sustainability of underground tourism by maintaining a sustainable visitor level, within current thresholds.

In other words, investment is needed to build infrastructure and collateral activities around the Castellana Caves; such investments should not be altogether separate from the main tourist attraction but serve to enhance it and support its development. Further, it should not distort or contaminate the natural environment in which the caves are located, but enhance it harmoniously, thereby ensuring that visitors have a pleasant experience that meets their expectations.

Attracting investment to support the Castellana Caves will require medium- to long-term strategic planning in the political-administrative field. This planning should concern both investments to improve the operations and management of Grotte di Castellana and, as previously mentioned, to protect the environment and develop supporting infrastructure for the tourist attraction. As regards the internal administration of Grotte di Castellana, it would be desirable for the company to modernise their operations in order to improve efficiency. For instance, they should seek to digitise their assets, appropriately train employees and, at the same time, implement a new culture of work and responsibilities in order to improve visitor reception, morality among the employees (who are essentially guides), the relationship between employees and the administration and, above all else, the external image of the caves. In particular, any training or recruitment of guides should prioritise the ability to provide assistance in a foreign language, in addition to the implementation of digital techniques.

If an ambitious policy of infrastructural investment and environmental redevelopment of the area surrounding the karst compound were to be initiated, it would likely attract investors and sponsors, due to the cave complex's significant promotional and income prospects; this would then trigger a virtuous cycle that would generate additional income flows – for the managing company, the investors and the municipality. The initial funds needed to plan and begin infrastructural development could stem from Grotte di Castellana's annual payment to the municipality; it would be reasonable for part of this fee to be earmarked for a fund aimed at financing – together with additional public and private funds – urban and environmental redevelopment works in the area around the caves. As mentioned, once this process begins, there will likely be many opportunities to attract external investors, as there are several public and private asset management companies that specialise in the management of investment funds aimed at enhancing real estate or public environmental assets.

Finally, with regard to the ownership structure and governance model of Grotte di Castellana, there is an urgent need to institutionally and operationally increase the administrative and managerial freedom of the corporate board. In this sense, we cannot ignore the serious and concrete risk that a rigid, and in some ways short-sighted interpretation and application of the legislation on in-house companies may compromise the autonomy of the managing company and limit its operating margins. Over time, such a compromise will inevitably lead to a reduction in business volume and therefore the bankruptcy of the investee company – in this case, Grotte di Castellana.

Budget analysis

Before analysing a company's economic and financial performance, it is necessary to first review its corporate mission and management objectives, because any conclusions that are drawn from the financial accounts cannot be separated from these fundamental aspects. Formally, the mission of Grotte di Castellana is defined, as previously highlighted, in Article 3 of its Articles of Association, which defines its corporate purpose in a detailed and extensive manner. In line with its legal form as a joint stock company, the company pursues a 'hybrid' aim. On the one hand, it seeks to manage the karstic site in an optimal and efficient way, promoting it and enhancing it for tourism and acting on it in an environmentally sustainable way. On the other hand, its main aim of promoting and enhancing the tourism value of the cave compound is compromised by its partial public ownership, which limits its strategies and management, inhibits the autonomy of its managers and directs the company mission towards an 'almost mutualistic' end, in defiance of its joint stock company form. As the company is not a cooperative, but a limited liability company (and therefore joint stock), it is not appropriate for it to be oriented towards mutualistic purposes; however, in practice, it cannot be claimed that the company fully pursues the goal of profit, as its pursuit of this end is – as mentioned – contaminated and limited. This is because the public ownership of the company influences its management, directing it not towards profit maximisation but towards providing employment opportunities to the residents of Castellana Grotte and financially contributing to local social events, thereby improving the economic conditions of the local community.

During the first five years after the commercial launch (2000–2004), Grotte di Castellana was less oriented towards commercial development and more focused on environmental protection. Despite this, it enjoyed substantial economic and financial equilibrium. However, in 2003, it began to show declining turnover and an initial worsening of the conditions of economic equilibrium, and this began a period of difficulty, characterised by stable or reduced production and significant annual losses. However, in 2008, the company re-oriented to focus on commercial promotion of the karst site and the development of tourist events, and this interrupted the previous cycle of economic and equity imbalance. That year, turnover increased 18.46%. From then onwards, the company continued in its strategy of promoting tourism with increased conviction, and no longer showed signs of economic imbalance; rather, it entered a period of steady growth that progressively improved its asset solidity over time. In particular, starting in 2013, the company entered a five-year period of significant and constant growth in production, leading to its highest recorded turnover in the last financial year.

Contribution of the Castellana Caves to tourism and the local and regional economies

As highlighted above, each year, the Castellana Caves attract hundreds of thousands of tourists from all over the world, and, since their discovery to the present day, they have accommodated more than 17 million. This impressive tourist flow has generated, over the caves' 80-year history, a volume of direct business (i.e. revenues generated directly from cave visits) of more than 80 million euros, of which almost 65% has been generated in the past 18 years (since the establishment of Grotte di Castellana) and the remaining 35% generated in the prior 61 years.

These statistics are a testament to Grotte di Castellana's successful promotion and development of tourism to the hypogeous compound. The flow of tourists to the caves generates direct cash flows for the Municipality of Castellana Grotte through the defined annual fee (i.e. 30.19% of revenues), as well as obvious and clear indirect economic returns for the territory by increasing demand for local products and services and creating new opportunities for employment. Since their discovery, the caves have allowed entire generations of Castellanesi to earn income in levels that are otherwise uncommon in southern Italy; they have also encouraged the proliferation of business activities in the hospitality, catering and commerce sectors, thereby contributing to regional economic and social development. This impact is made particularly evident by an analysis of the growth in per capita income of the residents of Castellana Grotte between 2000 (i.e. Grotte di Castellana's first year of operation) to 2017, which can be inferred from the published data of the Ministry of Economy and Finance (MEF).[8] Specifically, over this period, the per capita income of local residents grew more (88.38%) than the regional (85.51%) and national (68.09%) averages, although its real value remained below the regional and national averages.

Historically, the flow of visitors to the Castellana Caves has demonstrated by high seasonality. Data on the monthly distribution of visitors to the caves, from 2000 to today, show that, on average, almost 59% of annual visitors arrive in the four summer months, demonstrating the significant influence of the seaside tourism of neighbouring municipalities.[9]

To analyse tourist flows in the Castellana Caves region over the period of 2005–2017, incoming tourist flows, tourist presence in accommodation sites,[10] average length of stay of tourists and internationalisation in Castellana Grotte (as well as neighbouring municipalities and the provincial capitals of Puglia) were analysed.[11]

From this analysis, it emerged that the Castellana Grotte, thanks to the fundamental contribution of its caves, recorded higher growth in incoming tourist flows (94.98%) than the regional average (57.16%) and – in the years 2008–2017 – significantly higher growth (102.64%) compared to the regional (33.86%) and national (27.90%) averages. This stellar performance is highlighted when we consider data on the presence (i.e. number of overnight stays) of tourists, which show that, in the 13-year period, overnight stays of tourists near the Castellana Caves increased by 126.19%, against the regional average of 40.12%. In general, in the period considered, excellent performance in terms of the arrivals and presence of tourists – which significantly exceed regional and national averages – were recorded by almost all neighbouring towns, with Alberobello, Valle d'Itria and seaside towns showing the best performance. This demonstrates how the area surrounding the Castellana Caves is of particular tourist appeal, and therefore offers excellent opportunities for collaboration through integrated tourism.

Even the average stay of tourists in Castellana Grotte (2.2 days in 2017), while significantly below the regional (3.88 days) and national (3.49 days) averages, increased 16% over the period, while the regional average reduced (−10.84%). However, the data on internationalisation are less positive, showing – as highlighted earlier – that there is much work to be done to pro-mote the hypogeum site internationally and to serve foreign tourists well, as only 16.47% of tourists who stayed overnight in 2017 at Castellana Grotte were foreigners, against a regional average of 23.26% and peaks of 45.70% in Alberobello and more than 30% in neighbouring seaside resorts.

It is therefore possible to affirm that, by exploiting a recent growth trend in tourism to Puglia – driven above all by the bathing sites of Salento and Gargano – Castellana Grotte, thanks to its hypogeum compound, and its neighbouring municipalities (especially Alberobello, Fasano, Polignano a Mare, Monopoli, Locorotondo and Martina Franca) has intercepted a good portion of tourists who are attracted by the Puglia 'brand'. However, it would be useful to understand if this tourist growth (and subsequent economic growth), has been accompanied by appropriate investments in human capital and infrastructure, aimed at raising the quality of services and accommoda-tion. Only in this way can the municipality hope to extend the trend of growing tourism; otherwise, as soon as the Puglia brand starts to lose its appeal, the localities and attractions mentioned earlier will pay the consequences.

A look to the future

The Castellana Caves are the most visited tourist attraction in Puglia, and among the top 20 attractions in Italy, which otherwise enjoys more than 8,000 paid tourist attractions and a natural heritage of inestimable value. Each year, the caves attract hundreds of thousands of tourists from across the world, and, since their discovery to the present day, they have accommodated more than 17 million. This impressive tourist flow has generated, over the caves' 80-year history, a volume of direct business (i.e. revenues earned directly from cave visits) of more than 80 million euros, of which almost 65% has been generated in the past 18 years (since the establishment of Grotte di Castellana) and the remaining 35% generated in the prior 61 years. This shows how Grotte di Castellana provided a fundamental impulse for the promotion and develop-ment of tourism to this hypogeum compound.

The flow of tourists to the caves generates direct cash flows for the Municipality of Castellana Grotte through the defined annual fee (i.e. 30.19% of revenues) as well as obvious and clear indirect economic returns for the region by increasing demand for local products and services and generating new opportunities for employment. Since their discovery, the caves have enabled entire generations of Castellanesi to earn income in levels that are otherwise uncommon in southern Italy; they have also encouraged the pro-liferation of local business activities in hospitality, catering and commerce, thereby contributing to regional economic and social development. It is also possible to affirm that, especially in the last five years, by exploiting the recent and extraordinary growth trend in tourism to Puglia, the Castellana Caves have intercepted a good portion of tourists who are attracted by the Puglia 'brand'. However, it would be useful to understand whether this tourist (and subsequent economic) growth has been accompanied by appropriate investments in human capital, organisational development and infrastructure, or if the company still demonstrates a model of tourism and employment that significantly driven by the bottom (i.e. low paid and low skilled service jobs). Only by investing in training – and therefore the quality of service provided – can the Castellana Caves hope to extend the current growth trends in tourism, intercepting the anticipated flows of Chinese tourists who have not yet fully discovered the wonders of Puglia. Otherwise, as soon as the Puglia brand starts to lose its appeal, even the Castellana Caves will risk paying the consequences.

In this concluding section, we look to the future, analysing aspects we consider fundamental for the future development of the Castellana Caves, as well as their surrounding region.

In this regard, we cannot fail to start from the company's social mission and governance model, as these are aspects of fundamental strategic importance in influencing company dynamics.

Formally, the mission of Grotte di Castellana is defined, as previously highlighted, in Article 3 of its Articles of Association, which defines its corporate purpose in a detailed and extensive manner. In line with its legal form as a joint stock company, the company pursues a 'hybrid' aim. On the one hand, it seeks to manage the karstic site in an optimal and efficient way, promoting it and enhancing it for tourism and acting on it in an environmentally sustainable way. On the other hand, its main aim of promoting and enhancing the tourism value of the cave compound is compromised by its partial public ownership, which limits its strategies and management, inhibits the autonomy of its managers and directs the company mission towards an 'almost mutualistic' end, in defiance of its joint stock company form. As the company is not a cooperative, but a limited liability company (and therefore joint stock), it is not appropriate for it to be oriented towards mutualistic purposes; however, in practice, it cannot be claimed that the company fully pursues the goal of profit, as its pursuit of this end is – as mentioned – contaminated and limited. This is because the public ownership of the company influences its management, directing it not towards profit maximisation but towards providing employment opportunities to the residents of Castellana Grotte and financially contributing to local social events, thereby improving the economic conditions of the local community.

The company's ownership structure and governance model thereby influence its social mission and, at the same time, generate conditions of extreme administrative instability. This inevitably limits its managerial independence, binding administrators to the short term, only, as dictated by local political cycles. The resulting situation is prone to halt the development of investment policies in human, organisational and infrastructural capital, which often require several years to bear fruit, with obvious implications for management performance and economic and financial results. With regard to the ownership structure and consequent governance model, we cannot fail to point out the need to institutionally and operationally increase the administrative and managerial freedom of the senior management team. To this end, a possible solution could be to externally recruit a general manager with specific technical qualifications and sector experience; such a figure should be free from political appointments and identified by the Board of Directors through a comprehensive selection process drawing exclusively on meritocratic criteria. The appointee could have a temporally bound mandate aimed at organisational, tourist and commercial development of the caves, as well as their surrounding area.

The Board of Directors should maintain strategic oversight over and administrative responsibility for the corporate deeds, delegating operational and strategic responsibility to a general manager. The general manager should also play a consultative role for the Board. In this way, the goal of institutionally and operationally increasing the administrative and managerial freedom of top management, who would be subject to periodic evaluation and control of ownership, could be pursued. Such an arrangement would enable the management team to plan projects and evaluate results over a longer time horizon. Given this, it would be desirable to increase the director mandate to a term of four or five years, tying it to that of the general manager. Contrary to what has been proposed, however, we cannot ignore the serious and concrete risk that a rigid, and in some ways short-sighted interpretation and application of the legislation on in-house companies may compromise the autonomy of the managing company and limit its operating margins. Over time, such a compromise will inevitably lead to a reduction in business volume and therefore the bankruptcy of the investee company – in this case, Grotte di Castellana.

All of the abovementioned risks and opportunities have implications for the larger society, especially if reputational effects are taken into consideration. Modern tourists are more informed, attentive and demanding than ever before, and their propensity to communicate and transfer their impressions of an experience – for example over social media – is also much higher. Therefore, the reputational and economic risks involved in visitor dissatisfaction are significantly higher than in the past.

In this regard, it is necessary to highlight the logistical problems and consequent need for environmental, urban and architectural redevelopment of the area surrounding the karst compound. These criticalities inhibit the development of commercial and tourist activities related to the caves and, at the same time, are aesthetically displeasing to visitors. Substantial public and private investment is needed to connect the karst compound to the city centre and to other regional attractions. Similarly, environmental, urban and architectural redevelopment is needed to create an ideal environment for the development of collateral business activities, with respect to services, entertainment and accommodation; such activities would not only provide new employment opportunities, but would also attract public and private investment and thereby feed a virtuous cycle generating multiplier effects for regional production and income. These investments could be obtained from private and public parties, as well as the managing company (through investment of free capital reserves, in support of valorisation). Irrespective of its source, investment in infrastructure and services is needed to facilitate tourism and enhance the visitor experience, while also reducing the localisation and seasonality of the tourist flow and increasing tourists' average time spent in the region; all of these effects would have a profoundly positive impact on the regional entire economy.

The organisation of events or the creation of secondary tourist attractions near the caves – even outside the immediate area of Castellana – would be likely to attract visitors in the off-season, thus reducing the seasonality of tourist flows; this would not only facilitate the diversification of revenue sources, but it would also contribute to protecting the environmental sustainability of underground tourism by maintaining a sustainable visitor level, within current thresholds.

It will also be desirable for investment to be made in a variety of cultural events, including both permanent and 'out of season' events, to generate further media visibility for the caves and to promote secondary visitor attractions, which would incentivise tourists to prolong their stay in Castellana Grotte and neighbouring municipalities. Such events should be planned and promoted significantly in advance, to complement the behaviour of tourists from outside the region who plan their holidays months in advance. In particular, planning and promotion activities should be organised and implemented collaboratively with neighbouring municipalities, secondary tourist attractions and tourist accommodations, at least six months in advance, in order to provide a comprehensive billboard of local events and festivals.

In other words, investment is needed to build infrastructure and collateral activities around the Castellana Caves; such investments should not be altogether separate from the main tourist attraction but instead serve to enhance it and support its development. Relevant support structures may include accommodation facilities, restaurants, theme parks, museums, scientific and educational laboratories (open to tourists), amphitheatres, secondary tourist attractions, bookshops, local food and handicraft vendors, natural landscape attractions, sports facilities and entertainment venues. None of these entities should distort or contaminate the natural environment in which the cave is located, but each should enhance it harmoniously in order to improve the visitor experience.

The caves naturally offer visitors an experiential type of tourism, and this experiential aspect could be strengthened using appropriate initiatives. For instance, short questionnaires could be employed to determine visitors' opinions upon leaving the caves, in order to inform new initiatives for improving the visitor experience.

Attracting investment to support the Castellana Caves will require medium- to long-term strategic planning in the political-administrative field. This planning should concern both investments to improve the operations and management of Grotte di Castellana and, as previously mentioned, to protect the environment and develop supporting infrastructure for the tourist attraction. As regards the internal administration of Grotte di Castellana, it would be desirable for the company to modernise their operations in order to improve efficiency. For instance, they should seek to digitise their assets, appropriately train employees and, at the same time, implement a new culture of work and responsibilities in order to improve visitor reception, morality among the employees (who are essentially guides) and the relationship between employees and the administration. In these ways, the company should seek to implement – at all levels – a new culture of work and responsibility based on efficiency, productivity and effectiveness, in the interest of guaranteeing the best possible service. By doing so, it will remove the idea – often deep-rooted – that employment is a right (e.g. for political reasons), regardless of skill or the quality of the service rendered. The company must therefore invest in quality training for different levels of staff, while encouraging international experience. In particular, the training or recruitment of guides should prioritise the ability to provide assistance in a foreign language, as well as the implementation of digital techniques.

If an ambitious policy of infrastructural investment and environmental redevelopment of the area surrounding the karst compound were to be initiated, it would likely attract investors and sponsors, due to the cave complex's significant promotional and income prospects; this would then trigger a virtuous cycle that would generate additional income flows – for the managing company, the investors and the municipality. To this end, it would be worthwhile to create favourable commercial conditions for partnerships between the Castellana Caves and private companies, which could sponsor commercial initiatives in the caves area; use the external space for events, communication and promotion; obtain free entry for employees and customers; or acquire corporate gifts on advantageous terms.

The initial funds needed to plan and begin infrastructural development could stem from Grotte di Castellana's annual payment to the municipality; it would be reasonable for part of this fee to be earmarked for a fund aimed at financing – together with additional public and private funds – urban and environmental redevelopment works in the area around the caves. As mentioned, once this process begins, there will likely be many opportunities to attract external investors, as there are several public and private asset management companies that specialise in the management of investment funds aimed at enhancing real estate or public environmental assets. These investments would activate, also through the induced sector, a multiplicative cycle of further investment, production, employment and income for the region and its enterprises, which would increase the value of local buildings and revenues for the municipal coffers. But to start this process, a long-term vision and strategic planning is needed, accompanied by patience and courage to persist in meeting these objectives.

Notes

1 This section re-elaborates and interprets an interview with D'Orilia and a second interview with Alessandro Reina, researcher and professor of territorial geology at the Polytechnic of Bari, as well as Scientific Director of the Castellana Caves. Accordingly, the authors thank these informants for their precious collaboration. However, the content of this section, as well as the overall chapter, is obviously the sole responsibility of the author.

2 According to the AGTI, only natural underground cavities can be defined as tourist caves, in which – within precise opening periods and pre-established timetables – guided tours are organised along paths that are easily and safely walkable by anyone who is not affected by a particular physical handicap. Furthermore, access, always on payment, must be possible without the adoption of special equipment or speleological or mountain climbing clothing. Semi-tourist caves, in contrast, are defined as caves that can be visited and are equipped, but lack some of the abovementioned features and generally require personal lighting (preferably electric), which is often provided by the cave guides. Among the missing features, the most frequently lacking are an electrical system, accessible and safe paths and organised tours (Verole-Bozzello, 2014).

3 The content of this chapter is the sole responsibility of the authors; therefore, the persons mentioned are relieved of all responsibility for the considerations made, but thanked for their precious collaboration.

4 Franco Anelli, born in Lodi on 18 October 1899, graduated with a degree in the Natural Sciences at the University of Bologna in 1927 and worked for some years as a geologist in the Predil mines in Tarvisio. In 1930, he became a conservator at the Speleological Museum and an assistant at the Italian Institute of Speleology at the Postumia Caves. In 1938, he was commissioned by the Provincial Tourism Board of Bari to carry out a speleological survey in Puglia; through this survey, Anelli discovered unexplored caves and, on 23 January 1938, discovered (quite by chance) the Castellana Caves. These caves were destined to play a fundamental role in his future. In 1949, Anelli was called to Castellana to direct the caves – an assignment he continued until his death on 23 October 1977. Through this role, he devoted himself to intense exploration, surveying, scientific research and valorisation of the cavity as a tourist attraction. In 1940, thanks to Vito Matarrese (Anelli's collaborator since the time of discovery), the last and most beautiful cavern of the karst system of Castellana, the 'White Cave', was discovered.

5 In his first descent into the Castellana Caves – the base of which was covered by a vast amount of accumulated waste – Anelli reached the ground and identified a corridor that had been lost in the dark. Venturing inside and through a passage partially hidden by stalactite and stalagmitic concretions, he found himself in front of an exalted discovery: a large cavern, later called the 'Cave of Monuments', which was so wide that the beam of his lamp could not illuminate it in its entirety. In the following days, Anelli descended again into the Grave, accompanied by the Castellanese Vito Matarrese; together they continued their explorations and went inside for about 300 m, where they stopped at the end of a short descending gallery, now called the 'Corridoio del Serpente', in front of a deep well. Two months later, in March 1938, Anelli returned to Castellana and, together with Matarrese, continued his explorations, this time reaching more than 600 m beyond the Grave, where a new chasm, located in the current 'Corridoio del Deserto', arrested explorations again. During his brief stay in Castellana, Anelli began to

create the first relief of the caves, which he completed in September of the same year, during his third visit to Castellana. Anelli's explorations were continued by Matarrese, who, in 1940, overcame the Corridoio del Deserto chasm and reached the final known extent of the caves: the 'White Cave'.

6 In accordance with the company bylaws, these contributions pursue the aim of promoting the karst site regionally.

7 The legislation on in-house companies is defined in the testo unico delle società a partecipazione pubblica (i.e. DL No. 175 of 19 August 2016 and DL No. 100 of 16 June 2017), to which reference is made for a detailed analysis, as well as an appropriate critical analysis of the opportunity for Grotte di Castellana to be defined as an in-house company.

8 This indicator was calculated from MEF data using the ratio of the total amount of additional taxable income (IRPEF) of residents to the frequency (i.e. the number of residents declaring income and therefore recorded in the MEF statistics).

9 The days of greatest tourist influx at the karst site correspond to summer days on which adverse or uncertain weather conditions did not recommend to the use of nearby seaside resorts.

10 This refers to tourists who purchased and used local accommodation. By 'presence', we mean the sum of all days spent by each individual tourist.

11 It is probably superfluous to point out that the analysis was based on official data provided by ISTAT and the Puglia Region, although we are aware that, also due to the proliferation of bed and breakfasts and holiday homes, some transactions and tourist flows could escape the official data and therefore invalidate the significance of the analysis.

References

Grotte Di Castellana, *Reports and financial statements from 2000 to 2017*.

Verole-Bozzello V. (2014), *Testo per la preparazione professionale delle guide turistiche*, Associazione Grotte Turistiche Italiane, Società Speleologica Italiana.

6 Heritage assets as a cultural and tourist resource

The cases of the Pinacoteca di Brera, the National Archaeological Museum of Taranto and the RavennAntica Foundation

Introduction

The recent reorganisation of the Italian Ministry of Cultural Heritage and Activities and Tourism (MIBACT) occurred as a consequence of the spending review policies adopted in the period of 2012–2013 and implemented by DL No. 66 of 24 April 2014, according to which each Ministry was required to have new rules of organisation to incorporate reductions in organic plant. In implementing this internal reorganisation, MIBACT focused mainly on achieving equal dignity between the protection and enhancement of cultural heritage and landscape assets, the creation of a national museum system, the managerial and scientific autonomy of museums and archaeological parks, education and research, the research of new forms of management and the overturning of an elitist vision of culture. The aim, in fact, was to remedy some of the problems that had long plagued the administration of cultural heritage and tourism in Italy, including the lack of integration between the areas of culture and tourism, the general lag in innovation and training policies and the lack of autonomy of museums. Prior to the reform, museum directors had no effective autonomy; they represented, except in very isolated cases, no more than individual articulations of the superintendents. The MIBACT reorganisation, however, provided for:

- a new Directorate General for Museums, to which it entrusted the development of national policies and strategies and the tasks of enhancing the value of institutes and cultural places and drafting guidelines for entrance fees and museum services;
- the creation of 17 regional museum centres (i.e. peripheral branches of the Directorate General for Museums, responsible for promoting the enhancement agreements provided for by the Code of Cultural Heritage

and Landscape and for encouraging the creation of a museum system between state and non-state museums, both public and private);

• the assignment of the title of '*Ufficio Dirigenziale*' ('Executive Office') to 20 museums and archaeological sites of major national interest, giving them the highest administrative status, with directors – including foreign directors – who are publicly selected from within or outside the public administration.

In the light of the reorganisation of the Italian museum system, this chapter examines the contribution of museums – in their dual role as cultural heritage assets and tourist attractions – to local development, highlighting the extent to which they represent an important economic resource at regional level. To this end, the cases of the Pinacoteca di Brera, the National Archaeological Museum of Taranto (MArTA) and the RavennAntica Foundation (responsible for managing part of the cultural heritage of the municipality of Ravenna, including several museums) are analysed. These cases differ significantly in terms of their governance, geographical location, and socio-economic context, although they are in some ways complementary. The Pinacoteca di Brera is, in fact, an interesting example of Italy's national museum scene. The museum is located in Milan – one of the largest, most economically advanced and internationally opened cities in Italy. MArTA, instead, is a museum that is currently relaunching. It is situated in Taranto, a city of south of Italy with a problematic socio-economic context but great tourism potential. Finally, the Fondazione RavennAntica is a public–private organisation operating in the economically and culturally dynamic city of Ravenna (northeast of Italy). The heterogeneity of these heritage assets enables a particularly interesting comparison to be drawn with respect to the contribution of each to the local development, in terms of the flows of cultural tourism.

The analysis founds on a survey carried out between May and August 2018, which involved semi-structured interviews with the managers of each institution, investigating the management aspects of their respective organisations in terms of: strategic objectives, commercial development strategies and promotion, results achieved, innovations adopted and importance placed on environmental sustainability. Information collected were then cross-referenced with statistical data from secondary sources, as described in the following sections.[1]

Pinacoteca di Brera

Description

The Pinacoteca di Brera is a national gallery of ancient and modern art, located in the Brera Palace which is one of the largest complexes in Milan, covering more than 24,000 m². The origin of the Pinacoteca as a heterogeneous collection of works can be traced back to 1776, although it was only officially established in 1809. Situated next to the Brera Academy, it was founded for essentially educational purposes, commissioned by Maria Theresa of Austria with the aim of creating a collection of exemplary works that would be useful for training the nearby students. When Milan became the capital of the Kingdom of Italy, the collection was transformed into a museum by Napoleon, who wanted to exhibit the most significant paintings from the territories conquered by the French armies. The best works were, in fact, sent to Paris, while the remaining works were installed in picture galleries in the main cities of the Kingdom. Thus, the galleries of Venice, Bologna and Milan were born, with the latter hosting the compendium of artistic production in the Kingdom of Italy. In the Pinacoteca, the majority of the works on display originated in churches and monasteries, which justifies the prevalence of sacred paintings – often in large format – that gives the museum a particular physiognomy. The Pinacoteca, therefore, was not born from a private collection, as is the case of many great Italian museums (e.g. the Uffizi Gallery), but from political and state collections. The large Brera Palace also houses the Braidense National Library, the Brera Observatory, the Botanical Garden, the Lombard Institute of Science and Literature and the Academy of Fine Arts. The name 'Brera' derives from the fact that this palace was built on uncultivated land, or *braida* (alternatively, *breda* – a word that, in low Latinity, referred to a suburban field), and this inspired the name of both the palace and the entire neighbourhood in which it stands.

Today, the Pinacoteca is an internationally prominent museum that exhibits one of the most famous painting collections in Italy. It is particularly renowned for its Venetian and Lombard works, but the collection also includes important pieces from other schools. Among its masterpieces of Italian and foreign artists from the fourteenth to the nineteenth centuries are works by Piero della Francesca (the Montefeltro altarpiece), Andrea Mantegna (*Christ Died*), Raphael (*The Marriage of the Virgin*), Bramante (*Christ at the Column*) and Caravaggio (*The Dinner in Emmaus*), as well as Tintoretto, Giovanni Bellini, Rubens, Van Dyck and Francesco Hayez. In the 1970s and 1980s, the collection also included paintings and sculptures from the twentieth century, including masterpieces by Picasso, Boccioni, Modigliani, Arturo Martini, Marino Marini, Morandi, Carrà and de Pisis. In the courtyard leading to the Brera Palace, there is also an exhibition of Napoleon's bronze as Mars Pacifier, by Antonio Canova, which was commissioned by the Viceroy Eugenio de Beauharnais from the original marble. If we exclude the presence of this bronze and some statues of the greatest intellectuals and personalities of Milan (including the monument to Cesare Beccaria by Pompeo Marchesi and that to Giuseppe Parini by Gaetano Matteo Monti) – which are also exhibited in the palace's courtyard – the Pinacoteca di Brera is evidently a museum dedicated to paintings. While the collection also includes a number of drawings, these are not normally on display, but accessible only to scholars; the drawings include two by Leonardo da Vinci and two important preparatory cartoons by Guido Reni and Ludovico Carracci.

Governance

The Pinacoteca di Brera obtained its first level executive office qualification following the recent reform. Accordingly, its governance is led by the Director Pro Tempore, who is supported by the Board of Directors and the Scientific Committee (of which the Director is also Chairman), which represent purely advisory bodies. This mixture of roles, while streamlining the management of the Pinacoteca, leaves the responsibility for all decisions to the Director, alone.

The Pinacoteca's main management objectives form part of the declaration of competence of the Director, who is required to have a management quali-fication, as established by Article 35 of the Prime Minister's Decree No. 171 of 29 August 2014.[2] In this context, the mission of the Pinacoteca is to bring the museum as close as possible to the local residents, and vice versa; this is summarised in a very effective mission statement: 'to place the Pinacoteca in the heart of Milan and place visitors in the heart of the Pinacoteca'.

The objectives stated in this mission statement are, in fact, the two main strategic objectives pursued, to the extent that all decisions and actions are designed to achieve them. To this end, a three-year strategic plan was recently developed. The Director has discussed this plan with the Board of Directors and the Scientific Committee, and it has been sent to MIBACT for final approval.

As far as the first strategic objective is concerned ('placing the Pinacoteca in the heart of Milan'), the management approach seems quite far from the idea of transforming the museum into a driver of local growth (which is already very sustained) via cultural tourism. In fact, the objective does not emphasise tourism or tourists, but the cultural heritage of the gallery, which is considered to benefit the local community. Far from being an active target for growth, tourism is, on the contrary, conceived of as a consequence of proper museum management. In other words, the management approach sees cultural tourism – especially quality tourism – a by-product of achieving the strategic objective of making the Pinacoteca the most loved museum in the city and its cultural centre.

The analysis also shows a different approach to cultural tourism depending on whether it is generalist or return. Generalist tourism describes tourists making their first visit to a city and who want to learn about its cultural heri-tage and landscape; such tourists devote themselves to the enjoyment of the most important museums, monuments and sites. This is a very capricious type of tourism, because it is linked to factors that are external to the management and quality of the tourist attractions, themselves (e.g. exchange rate, terrorism warnings). Return tourism, on the other hand, occurs when tourists return to a city they have already visited and approach it as an 'insider' – as a resident – seeking to deepen their knowledge. In this respect, the management objective of the Pinacoteca is to focus on the second category of cultural tourists who show a greater propensity to spend. Thus, it could be said that the vision of the Pinacoteca is to focus primarily on very high-quality cultural tourism and to devote less space to generalist tourism. Milan is an ideal city in which to achieve this strategic goal, since – unlike other Italian cultural cities (e.g. Rome or Florence) – it is characterised by predominantly recurring tourism. The results achieved by the Pinacoteca seem to validate its strategic approach. In fact, the Pinacoteca is a museum that is much loved by the city and well positioned in terms of high-quality cultural tourism.

With regard to the second strategic objective ('placing visitors in the heart of the Pinacoteca'), the management team has focused on:

- capturing statistics on visitors in order to better orient the museum to their nature and preferences;
- introducing evening visits;
- abolishing temporary exhibitions, as these are expensive and tend to 'cannibalise' other museum activities;
- introducing 'dialogues' around one or two works borrowed from other museums.

The above shows that the innovations introduced by the Pinacoteca have mainly been based on the museum experience and quality. Furthermore, the innovations have been mainly incremental, and it cannot be inferred whether they were top-down or bottom-up. The analysis does not reveal the implementation of technological or marketing innovations. The Pinacoteca offer is certainly oriented to visitors, but with the sole objective of increasing museum accessibility. At the same time, the issue of environmental sustainability seems quite prevalent in managerial considerations, which have led to a series of initiatives aimed at energy saving, such as the installation of low consumption LED bulbs in all lighting equipment.

SWOT analysis

In this section we analyse – by means of a SWOT analysis – the strengths, weaknesses, opportunities and threats that concern the management of the Pinacoteca. The analysis takes into account both the internal environment (in terms of strengths and weaknesses) and the external environment (in terms of threats and opportunities). The results are shown in Figure 6.1.

With regard to the internal environment, the main strengths that emerged from the analysis are: mitigated autonomy over the budget, more autonomous governance (note that both aspects are a consequence of the recent reform) and the greater competence and qualifications of Pinacoteca staff. On the other hand, the main weakness is the lack of autonomy over human resources, which makes the project unsustainable from both governance and economic perspectives. As far as the external environment is concerned, two opportunities emerged: increasing the accessibility of the Pinacoteca and increasing donations from private individuals (which represents a great opportunity in terms of the budget). The greatest threat, on the other hand, is the uncertainty

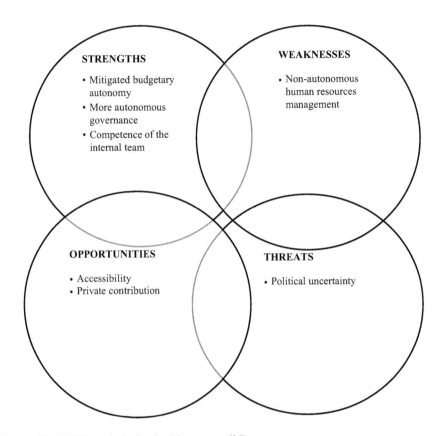

Figure 6.1 SWOT analysis for the Pinacoteca di Brera.

of the Italian political framework – a threat that will only fade if the museum becomes completely autonomous in its governance. On the other hand, any reduction in revenues (deriving from ticketing, events or concession fees) is not perceived as a real threat, as it is instead considered an aspect of normal risk management.

Data analysis

The socio-economic context of the Pinacoteca is one of Italy's largest, richest and most dynamic and productive cities. Milan covers an area of more than 180 km², with a population of nearly 1.4 million (and more than 3.2 million in its greater metropolitan area) at a density of 7,538.21 inhabitants per km² (http://dati.istat.it/). In 2016, the municipality calculated a value added per inhabitant of 46,441 euros; this is decidedly higher than the average for the region (32,860) and the northwest (30,574), and almost double that of the Italian provinces (24,884). The municipality also demonstrates excellent performance in terms of employment, with an unemployment rate of 6.2% in 2016; this rate was lower than the equivalent rate at the provincial (7.5%), regional (7.4%), northwest (8.1%) and national (11.7%) levels (http://dati. comune.milano.it/; http://dati.istat.it/).

From a touristic point of view, Milan is one of the most visited Italian cities and, in 2016, ranked 6th on the list of the most visited cities in Europe and 14th in the world (Global Destination Cities Index, 2017). The economic value of international tourism in Milan is confirmed by the city's foreign tourist arrivals (3,248,525 in 2016) and presences (7,085,826), which are systematically higher than that of domestic tourists (1,839,998 and 3,890,658, respectively), suggesting the important role played by tourism in Milan in determining the volume of Italian exports. However, the average stay of tourists in Milan is low, as it never exceeds 2.5 nights for foreign tourists (and 2.1 for domestic tourists) (http://dati.comune.milano.it/). Despite this, tourists in Milan can count on a generous accommodation capacity, as the number of institutions offering accommodation has roughly tripled in recent years, from 835 in 2006 to more than 2,400 in 2016 (http://dati.istat.it/). This corresponds to an increase in the number of beds from approximately 75,000 to 97,000 in the same period. One stimulus for this growth trend has been the rise in complementary businesses – particularly hostels and bed & breakfasts.

The socio-economic and touristic context outlined earlier frames the performance of the Pinacoteca and its contribution to the local economy, in terms of flows of cultural tourism. In this regard, it should be noted that, from a cultural point of view, Milan is an extremely lively and dynamic city. Its long literary, artistic, musical and scientific tradition has made it a driving force and crossroads of culture, and numerous traces of this tradition are preserved in important museum collections, including that of the Pinacoteca. In recent years (with the exception of 2014), the Pinacoteca was firmly placed in the top 20 of the most visited cultural sites in Italy. In terms of attendance and revenues, the museum has recorded, in recent years, a stable increase in visitors and revenues, with both representing approximately 20% of those at the regional level (Table 6.1).

In particular, the average number of annual visitors was approximately 270,000 in the period 2011–2014, before increasing significantly to almost 365,000 in 2017. The same trend applied to revenues, which rose from an average of approximately 750,000 euros in the period 2011–2014 to almost 1,800,000 in 2017.

MArTA

Description

MArTA is one of the most important museums in southern Italy, with one of the largest collections of Magna Graecia artefacts. The museum was founded in 1887 with a deposit of antiquities by the state administration and, since

Table 6.1 Visitors and revenue of the Pinacoteca di Brera, 2011–2016 (www.statistica.beniculturali.it)

		Paying	Not paying	Total visitors	Gross income (€)	Net income (€)
2011	Brera	154,674	132,716	**287,390**	745,148.00	**670,633.20**
	Lombardy	808,411	606,409	1,414,820	4,252,710.50	3,785,228.46
	Italy	17,230,236	23,993,398	41,223,634	117,008,677.42	94,067,373.55
2012	Brera	158,820	106,598	**265,418**	889,698.00	**800,728.20**
	Lombardy	821,082	550,563	1,371,645	4,342,140.75	3,922,290.21
	Italy	16,800,917	20,397,878	37,198,795	118,511,857.83	96,721,185.80
2013	Brera	146,883	102,696	**249,579**	826,800.00	**744,120.00**
	Lombardy	852,967	587,322	1,440,289	4,561,523.25	4,113,289.94
	Italy	17,649,829	20,774,758	38,424,587	126,417,467.38	104,268,818.17
2014	Brera	160,570	109,235	**269,805**	882,866.20	**794,579.58**
	Lombardy	919,626	580,790	1,500,416	5,003,515.20	4,496,179.94
	Italy	19,070,256	21,674,507	40,744,763	135,510,701.74	111,807,913.64
2015	Brera	186,769	135,603	**322,372**	1,037,312.00	**933,580.80**
	Lombardy	1,012,170	640,428	1,652,598	5,986,736.50	5,312,874.80
	Italy	20,768,279	23,023,883	43,792,162	155,494,414.89	125,220,424.42
2016	Brera	212,919	130,254	**343,173**	1,812,604.20	**1,631,343.78**
	Lombardy	1,111,069	721,399	1,832,468	7,993,159.35	7,059,450.87
	Italy	22,565,617	22,818,256	45,383,873	173,440,743.76	138,477,635.01
2017	Brera	221,313	143,228	**364,541**	1,981,491.00	**1,783,341.90**
	Lombardy	1,076,485	777,077	1,853,562	9,194,747.90	8,136,645.81
	Italy	24,068,632	26,194,888	50,263,520	193,915,670.96	156,033,331.81

that time, it has occupied the former convent of the Friars Alcantarini (or San Pasquale). The structure was built shortly after the middle of the eighteenth century and modified and enlarged several times after 1901, when the facades were rebuilt and a northern wing was added. The discoveries made in Apulia at the time of the Kingdom of the Two Sicilies were, at that time, in the collections of the Royal Bourbon Museum of Naples and the Museum of Lecce – the oldest institution in the region. At that time, private individuals could exercise their right of ownership over objects found underground, even carrying out unauthorised excavations with the sole purpose of sourcing artefacts for their private collections. With the improvement in legislative structures and the ability of some archaeologists to relate with notables of the city, donations of important artefacts to museums increased, thereby expanding archaeological collections. Today, the increase in artefacts in museum collections is mainly driven by excavations carried out by superintendents and, albeit secondarily, by the purchase of private collections over which MIBACT exercises the right of first refusal.

Due to the need to adapt the structure and systems of the convent building and the need to rationalise the collections on display, the museum's exhibition itinerary was reduced in 1998, leading to the complete closure of the museum to the public at the beginning of 2000 (persisting until the end of 2007). The museum was re-opened to the public on 21 December 2007, when it was officially renamed with its current acronym, 'MArTA'.

As regards the exhibition route, the ground floor of the museum building currently houses offices and laboratories, the 'Meeting Room' and spaces for temporary exhibitions, as well as spaces for receiving visitors. The permanent exhibition is located on the two upper floors and a new mezzanine floor, and is organised around the most significant aspects of the ancient population of the local area of Taranto within wide chronological bands, starting from the first evidence of life in the fifth millennium BC to late antiquity and the early medieval period. Ample space is given to the phases of Spartan colonisation on the coasts of the Gulf of Taranto, the cults, the economy, the funeral rituals of the Greek city and the relations between Hellenic culture and the indigenous world.

Today, MArTA is one of the most active and appreciated museums in Italy, and ranks third among the 23 most visited cultural sites in Apulia, behind Castel del Monte and Castello Svevo.

Governance

Similar to other museums with executive office qualifications, MArTA enjoys mitigated managerial, financial and scientific autonomy. Its governance is articulated in the figure of the Director Pro Tempore, who is supported by the Board of Directors and the Scientific Committee (both purely consultative bodies), as well as the Board of Auditors (the only control body). Within this structure, the Director has immediate and total control over safety matters only, as all staff are directly employed by MIBACT. The analysis shows that this form of governance – which has long characterised Europe's most important museums – favours MArTA's mission, despite its peripheral nature. To ensure maximum transparency, prevent mistakes and share the cultural and management policy widely, MArTA's management team works closely with the Board of Directors, the Scientific Committee and the Board of Auditors to ensure that the most important decisions are taken in a collegiate way, even in situations in which they could be established independently by the Director. These governing bodies were also decisive during the museum redesign (which occurred in December 2015), when it was necessary to take a series of decisions regarding the creation of offices, activities and strategic plans and to solve related problems.

Furthermore, MArTA's management objectives fall within the scope of the declaration set out in Article 35 of Prime Minister's Decree No. 171 of 29 August 2014. More specifically, the vision, orientation and strategies of the museum management are set out in a strategic plan that is organised according to five categories of objectives, relating to:

1. the management structure;
2. the collections and research policy;
3. scientific planning and publishing (temporary exhibitions and incentives to publish the results of the museum's scientific research);
4. the enhancement and use of heritage;
5. patronage and fundraising.

Within the strategic plan, a series of 'values' are identified that represent the following macro-objectives that MArTA intends to pursue:

- to encourage a 'territorial' project by transforming the museum not only into a centre for research, education, pedagogy and the conservation of goods, but also into a socio-cultural, tourist and economic flywheel for the region;
- to promote the identity link with cultural heritage that the municipality and province of Taranto have lost;
- to become an element of knowledge production, innovation, excellence and international design;
- to enhance the cultural relationship between Taranto and Magna Graecia, through the creation of a brand capable of fostering a connection with Basilicata and Calabria;
- to conceive archaeology as a stratification of not only sites and heritage, but also meanings, starting from Taranto as a city of culture;
- to encourage the theme of the value of the sea as a cultural element, transforming Taranto – now a city 'on the sea' – into a city 'of the sea';
- to promote the concept of a 'diffuse museum' as a territorial project, providing visitors with information on not only the provincial area, but also the regional and wider areas.

To date, the main results achieved have been:

- inclusion of the museum in the strategic tourism plan for Apulia, with the aim of enhancing tourist appeal;
- intense visitor profiling, with subsequent quantitative and qualitative analyses to improve knowledge on museum users;
- improvement of the visitor experience, in line with international standards;
- the introduction of a pricing policy that offers cultural activities at different rates;
- the creation of a cultural programme targeting various market segments, through a monthly calendar based on a macro-theme and divided into weekly events;[3]
- improved communication and promotion through a strategy that – despite the lack of a dedicated social media manager – has developed a strong social media presence;[4]
- the implementation of partnerships and networks and, therefore, integrated planning, through the stipulation of protocols of understanding and conventions with research centres, universities, schools, international laboratories and all stakeholders of excellence in the local area.[5]

MArTA's future management goals can be summarised in the following points:

- further enhancement of the museum's tourist appeal with possible benefits (in terms of tourist flow) for the municipality of Taranto;
- cooperation with institutional, economic and entrepreneurial actors in order to create tourist packages based on specific cultural itineraries;
- the inclusion of MArTA in tourism promotion and communication on social networks in order to integrate it with the territory to the extent that it becomes 'the' museum of Apulia (i.e. the most important museum in the region);
- transformation of the municipality of Taranto into an international laboratory through a reconversion of the city that is not only topographical and urbanistic, but above all cultural, taking as an example successful European cases such as Liverpool, Manchester and Bilbao;
- greater attention paid to patronage and fundraising, to which MArTA management has given only limited attention, due to a lack of human resources and specific know-how.

SWOT analysis

The results of the SWOT analysis for MArTA are presented in Figure 6.2.

As far as the internal environment is concerned, one of the main strengths identified by the analysis is the richness of the museum's archaeological heritage, which makes it very well known at national and international levels.

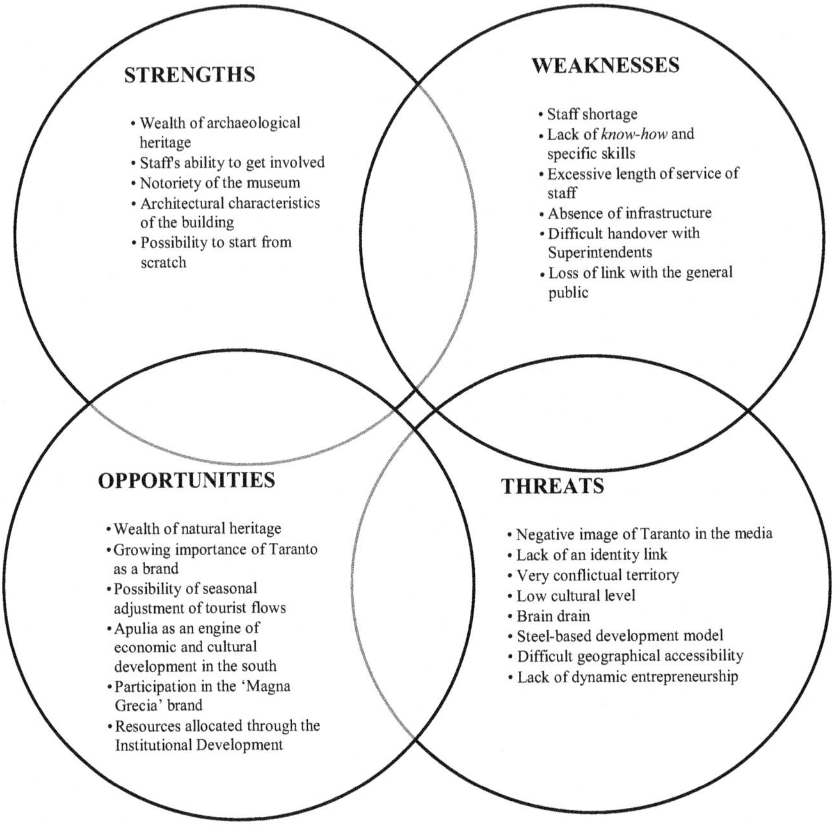

Figure 6.2 SWOT analysis for MArTA.

Despite the critical staffing issues discussed below, another strength is the flexibility of the staff, despite their excessive length of service. Other strengths include: the historically and architecturally relevance of the building (which helps to increase the museum's appeal) and the possibility for management to start from scratch. Although this last aspect may seem like a weakness, rather than a strength, it in fact represents an important incentive and a great stimulus to operate, enabling management to start from scratch a series of activities that did not previously exist.

One of the main weaknesses revealed by the survey is the serious staff shortage, as the museum currently counts only 53 employees (including the Director) compared to the 90 units they had planned. At the time of the museum re-opening, the staff was characterised by a lack of know-how: in particular, the curatorial sector was completely absent due to a lack of archaeologists and dedicated scientific staff; there was also a lack of specific expertise in accounting and no knowledge of foreign languages in support and supervision staff (as they had not been trained according to international standards). Another weakness identified in the analysis is the excessive length of service of most employees (many of whom are close to retirement). Moreover, furnishings do not guarantee the possibility of carrying out all planned activities. Likewise, the IT infrastructure is lacking updated software and hardware, with most computers older than 10 years or not functioning at all; combined with this, most staff have very low IT skills. Finally, some problems emerged in the handover from the superintendents due to warehouses that needed to be organised *ex novo*, following MArTA's many years of closure. It is precisely this last aspect that most determined MArTA's loss of ties with the community: the museum became very self-referential and communicated fundamentally to an audience of specialists, rather than the more generalist public, who came to perceive MArTA as a sort of 'ivory tower' rather than a 'home' for Taranto's residents, which it became only later.

As far as the external environment is concerned, MArTA's main opportunities include: the richness of the natural and cultural heritage; the growing importance of Taranto as a brand, both within Apulia and internationally; the nearby sea, which conveys a flow of foreign tourists even in non-summer months; the regional context, with Apulia considered the engine of southern Italy and among the most culturally dynamic regions; the context of the Mediterranean as a cultural and tourist asset; the strategic opportunity for MArTA's location between Lecce and Matera (the latter of which was named a European capital of culture in 2019) within multiple cultural and tourist routes; and the many resources that the municipality of Taranto has begun to invest in recent years.

Finally, as far as threats are concerned, the most relevant ones include: the negative image of Taranto in the media due to pollution; the lack of an identity link; the very factious, conflictual local context, which tends to destroy relations rather than build them, as well as demonstrating poor planning; a generally low to moderate cultural level; a brain drain; a development model that, for many years, has been based on steel production and has led to a lack of openness towards other production sectors; poor accessibility in the region, due to infrastructural problems (there are only two daily high-speed trains, sea transport is not sufficiently valued, etc.); and, finally, a lack of rich and dynamic entrepreneurship in the region, resulting in a lack of appropriate sponsorship.

Data analysis

MArTA's socio-economic context is that of a medium-sized town in southern Italy – Taranto – which had just under 200,000 inhabitants on 31 December 2017. Taranto is home to a large industrial and commercial port and an arsenal of the Italian Navy, as well as a naval station. The province records a fairly low value added per inhabitant (14,971 euros in 2015), in line with that of the Apulia Region (15,885), but lower than the average for southern Italy (16,333) and the nation (24,453) (http://dati.istat.it/). Moreover, compared to the overall nation, Taranto is in a much more deprived position, recording approximately 7,000 to 8,000 euros less in annual value added per inhabitant over the entire period of 2006–2016. However, despite the low levels of per capita income, Taranto's unemployment rate (16.8% in 2017) is lower than that of Apulia (18.8%) and Mezzogiorno (19.4%), although higher than the national average (11.2%) (http://dati.istat.it/). The unemployment problems are certainly exacerbated by the situation of ILVA – the largest steel plant in Europe, which closed in 2012 following serious environmental violations that led to hundreds of deaths. Since then, the state has engaged in a long and complicated process to attempt to revive the company, both to avoid the loss of thousands of jobs and to safeguard its contribution to the Italian economy.

From a touristic point of view, the town is located between Apulia and Basilicata's most important cities and is, therefore, at an important cross-roads for tourism flows across the two regions. Arrivals (87,482 in 2017) and presences (231,617) have increased in recent years, with arrivals representing approximately 30% of provincial arrivals in 2017 (289,468), though only slightly more than 2% of regional arrivals (3,911,688) (Pugliapromozione, 2018; http://dati.istat.it/). The data also suggest a fair number of foreign tourist arrivals (13,439 in 2017), although, in this case, the relative growth trend over recent years is less marked than that of Italian tourists. In particular, if we consider the entire area of Magna Graecia and Murgia, most of tourism flows in 2017 originate from Germany and France – the first with 4,432 arrivals and 18,310 overnight stays and the second with 5,279 arrivals and 17,727 over-night stays (www.agenziapugliapromozione.it/portal/). In the same year, the municipality of Taranto was ranked first for the number of arrivals (87,482) and second for overnight stays (231,617), though it recorded an average stay of only 2.6 nights, among the lowest in the area (Pugliapromozione, 2018). Taranto's growing demand for tourism is matched by an equally increasing trend in supply. In fact, the number of accommodation providers raised from 183 in 2006 to 759 in 2017, with a substantial increase in beds from 14,076 to 20,137 over the same period (http://dati.istat.it/).

From a cultural perspective, Taranto represents an important colony of Magna Graecia, with countless traces of historical and cultural monuments scattered throughout the city. Some of these traces include ancient places of worship, such as the remains of the Doric Temple; the archaeological Greco-Roman necropolis and chamber tombs; the Crypt of the Redeemer; and palaces that once belonged to noble families and illustrious personalities, such as the Palazzo Pantaleo and Palazzo d'Ayala Valva. The city also offers rich architectural variety in its religious artefacts, ranging from the Romanesque/Baroque facade of the cathedral of San Cataldo to the Gothic church of San Domenico Maggiore and much more elegant churches featuring Renaissance and neoclassical lines. Taranto also hosts the 'Alfredo Majorano' ethnographic museum, located in the Galeota Palace.

Within the socio-economic, touristic and cultural context outlined above, MArTA has registered, in recent years, a visible increase in visitors and revenues of, respectively, approximately 8% and 13% of the regional values (Table 6.2).

In particular, the number of visitors – which, from 2011–2015, stood at an average of 42,000 – almost doubled in 2016, reaching a total of more than 82,000. A similar trend was demonstrated for revenues, which grew from approximately 51,000 euros in 2006 to more than 156,000 in 2017.

RavennAntica Foundation

Description

The activity of the Parco Archeologico di Classe Foundation, known as 'RavennAntica', began at the end of October 2001 with the aim of enhancing, also for touristic purposes, the archaeological, architectural and historical-artistic heritage of the ancient city of Classe, the Basilica of Sant'Apollinare in Classe, the Domus of the 'Tappeti di Pietra' in Ravenna and the churches of Sant'Eufemia and San Nicolò.

As outlined on the foundation's official website (www.ravennantica.it), RavennAntica operates through framework agreements and/or agreements with the Regional Directorate for Cultural Heritage of Emilia-Romagna, the Superintendent for Archaeological Heritage of Emilia-Romagna, the Superintendent for Architectural Heritage of Ravenna and the University of Bologna. Through this framework, it promotes – with the contribution of the Fondazione del Monte di Bologna e Ravenna, excavation campaigns in the area surrounding the site of the ancient city of Classe, with the aim of creating a large archaeological park around the Basilica of Sant'Apollinare (recognised as a UNESCU World Heritage Site).

RavennAntica also promotes the restoration of artefacts – particularly mosaics – through its laboratory, which is destined to become a true centre of international excellence. In this context, the foundation has already conducted important projects in Syria. It also manages the important site of the Domus dei Tappeti di Pietra – returned to public use in 2002 – and promotes important scientific exhibitions, which have achieved great public success. Finally, RavennAntica is entrusted with the management of the Rasponi Crypt and the Hanging Gardens in the Provincial Administration Building of Ravenna.

Governance

The RavennAntica Foundation is a public–private organisation. The founding members are the municipality of Ravenna, the province of Ravenna, the Archdiocese of Ravenna Cervia, the University of Bologna and the Fondazione Cassa di Risparmio di Ravenna. All members are represented on

Table 6.2 MArTA visitors and revenues, 2011–2017 (www.statistica.beniculturali.it)

		Paying	Not paying	Total visitors	Gross income (€)	Net income (€)
2011	MArTA	**11,028**	**31,401**	**42,429**	**51,572.50**	**51,572.50**
	Apulia	190,882	369,096	559,978	560,294.75	560,294.75
	Italy	17,230,236	23,993,398	41,223,634	117,008,677.42	94,067,373.55
2012	MArTA	**9,306**	**28,886**	**38,192**	**42,109.00**	**42,109.00**
	Apulia	174,036	336,888	510,924	669,108.25	669,108.25
	Italy	16,800,917	20,397,878	37,198,795	118,511,857.83	96,721,185.80
2013	MArTA	**6,511**	**20,656**	**27,167**	**29,763.50**	**28,827.95**
	Apulia	187,382	328,724	516,106	728,311.50	727,375.95
	Italy	17,649,829	20,774,758	38,424,587	126,417,467.38	104,268,818.17
2014	MArTA	**16,989**	**30,867**	**47,856**	**73,638.50**	**53,756.11**
	Apulia	212,479	341,303	553,782	825,313.00	615,475.21
	Italy	19,070,256	21,674,507	40,744,763	135,510,701.74	111,807,913.64
2015	MArTA	**23,217**	**32,194**	**55,411**	**109,921.00**	**80,242.33**
	Apulia	284,095	307,122	591,217	1,190,167.25	870,916.75
	Italy	20,768,279	23,023,883	43,792,162	155,494,414.89	125,220,424.42
2016	MArTA	**37,381**	**44,938**	**82,319**	**176,369.00**	**128,749.37**
	Apulia	319,506	308,883	628,389	1,396,514.75	1,021,647.36
	Italy	22,565,617	22,818,256	45,383,873	173,440,743.76	138,477,635.01
2017	MArTA	**29,048**	**50,554**	**79,602**	**214,150.00**	**156,329.50**
	Apulia	256,615	493,678	750,293	1,574,920.50	1,151,697.80
	Italy	24,068,632	26,194,888	50,263,520	193,915,670.96	156,033,331.81

the Board of Directors. The assignment of management tasks, in furtherance of the programme objectives, are, on the other hand, entrusted to a Director General. The presence of both public and private subjects in the governing body enables RavennAntica to create strong relationships in the local area and to ensure the careful supervision of the managerial strategies.

The foundation's mission can be summarised in three points: (i) to guarantee the adequate conservation of the cultural goods conferred and/or given in concession; (ii) to improve the public consumption of these goods; and (iii) to realise forms of valorisation of the national and international mosaic patrimony, also through restoration of the goods. Moreover, RavennAntica's management is particularly attentive to requests from economic interlocutors and regularly meets with local trade organisations. RavennAntica has employed the following strategies to improve operations:

- providing integrated ticketing linked with the creation of monument circuits;[6]
- modulating opening hours according to seasonality and tourist flows (e.g. summer evening openings);
- developing programmes targeting different market segments, such as concerts, workshops and shows for children and conferences for the general public;
- creating and maintaining collaborations with local cultural institutions to realise shared events and integrated promotion;
- providing frequent guided tours for specific types of visitors, such as families with children, university teachers, etc.;
- combining social media communication with the use of traditional promotion methods, such as brochures and press releases;
- creating and promoting an association to support RavennAntica's activities.

To date, one of the main results achieved by RavennAntica is the renewed public enjoyment of important sites of cultural interest, such as the Domus dei Tappeti di Pietra (which has seen almost 900,000 visitors since 2002), the Complex of San Nicolò (with the realisation of seven major archaeological exhibitions in 7 years, and, since 2011, home to the museum 'TAMO. All the Adventures of the Mosaic') and the Ancient Port of Class. The inauguration of CLASSIS Ravenna, the new Museum of the City and the Territory, and the consequent creation of a new tourist and cultural circuit of the ancient city of Classe (later added to Ravenna's traditional monumental circuit), consisting of the museum, the archaeological site of the Ancient Port of Classe and the Basilica of Sant'Apollinare in Classe, is also planned for the near future. Another important result achieved is the significant increase in the number of visitors to managed monuments, including the Basilica of Sant'Apollinare in Classe, the Mausoleum of Theodoric and the National Museum (with the increase in visitors peaking at more than 30% in the first six months of 2018).

RavennAntica also recorded a significant increase in revenue from its own resources (ticket office and bookshop), which achieved a share of almost 50% in 2018.

Finally, the analysis highlighted the foundation's general managerial attention to environmental sustainability. RavennAntica's building works (first and foremost the restoration of the former sugar refinery that now houses the CLASSIS Ravenna museum) have always been carried out in compliance with the laws and directives on environmental protection, prioritising the use of eco-friendly materials.

SWOT analysis

The results of the SWOT analysis of the RavennAntica Foundation are presented in Figure 6.3.

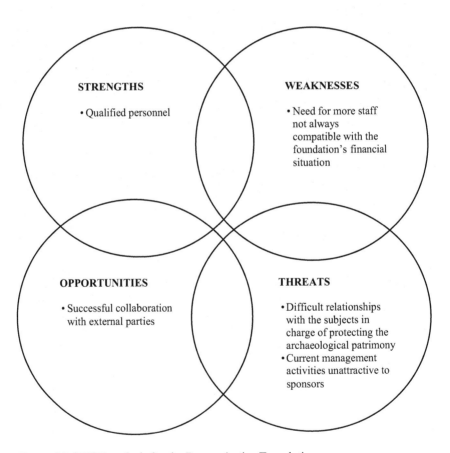

Figure 6.3 SWOT analysis for the RavennAntica Foundation.

The main strength identified by the analysis is the employment of qualified and skilled personnel in every organisational role. This has facilitated great managerial dynamism and provided strong motivation for growth and experimentation. The most significant weakness, on the other hand, is the fact that the particularly rapid growth has led, in recent years, to a greater need for personnel, which cannot always be met, depending on the foundation's financial situation; as a consequence, the operating structure is sometimes placed under stress.

As far as the external environment is concerned, the greatest opportunity comes from collaboration with stakeholders. However, some difficulties have been encountered with the parties responsible for protecting the archaeological heritage, who are not always willing to collaborate and are not necessarily devoted to enhancing the historical-artistic heritage. In addition, there have been some difficulties in financing day-to-day management activities, which, unlike 'special' projects, are less attractive to sponsors and difficult to fit into funding channels linked to European projects.

Data analysis

The socio-economic context in which the set of heritage assets managed by the RavennAntica Foundation is located is that of the municipality of Ravenna – a small to medium-sized city in northeast Italy, which had approximately 159,000 inhabitants on 31 December 2017. Ravenna is the largest and most historically important city in Romagna; its municipal territory is the second largest in Italy for surface area – surpassed only by that of Rome – and it includes nine shores of the Riviera Romagnola. The province of Ravenna registered a value added per inhabitant of 27,662.8 euros in 2015, slightly lower than the regional (30,242.1) and northeast (29,238.6) averages, but approximately 3,000 higher than the national average (24,453.7) (http://dati. istat.it/). Similarly, in 2017, the unemployment rate (7.2%) was higher than the average for the region (6.9%) and the northeast (6.3%), but lower than the national average (11.2%) (http://dati.istat.it/).

The municipality of Ravenna is very attractive from a touristic point of view. Beyond the presence of numerous cultural assets (discussed later), the city offers a remarkable variety of landscapes. In addition, its 30 km of coastline includes nine seaside resorts, each with its own peculiarities and suitable for every type of stay. The average number of arrivals in the province over the period 2010–2016 amounted to approximately 1.1 million, of which roughly 220,000 were foreign tourists (http://imprese.regione.emilia-romagna.it/turismo). Moreover, the average stay is between 4.5 and 5.5 days – driven, above all, by beach tourism. The tourist demand corresponds to a wide and varied supply that, in the municipality of Ravenna alone, included 1,749 accommodating structures in 2017, for a total of almost 77,000 beds (http://dati.istat. it/). Ravenna also offers a wide range of cultural tourist attractions, due to the presence of eight monuments included in the UNESCO World Heritage

List (the Mausoleum of Galla Placidia, the Orthodox Baptistery, the Aryan Baptistery, the Basilica of Sant'Apollinare Nuovo, the Chapel of Sant'Andrea in the Archiepiscopal Museum, the Mausoleum of Theodoric, the Basilica of San Vitale and the Basilica of Sant'Apollinare in Classe), along with other museums and cultural sites of historical, artistic and archaeological interest. All these cultural sites attract a flow of more than a million visits each year – mainly directed towards the 28 cultural sites located in the municipal area, which records almost 900,000 visits annually. The widespread nature of the city's cultural offer is accompanied by considerable managerial fragmentation that can be broken down into four main systems:

- state cultural sites;
- the ecclesiastical system;
- sites operated by RavennAntica Foundation;
- other museums and cultural sites that are managed by the municipality of Ravenna or private parties.

Ravenna's cultural tourism demonstrates seasonal dynamics, in moderate correlation with the seaside tourist market, with a greater concentration in the spring months (April and May), during which the component of the demand constituted by school groups is generally most concentrated. Visits to museums belonging to the RavennAntica circuit show a similar seasonal pattern, with an added bump in the summer due to seaside tourists, given the fair share of visits that the Domus and other nearby areas record in August and July.

Analysing the trend in demand at the foundation's sites (Tables 6.3 and 6.4), we can note a considerable increase in the number of visitors in the period 2003–2012, equivalent to an annual average growth rate of 6.9%.

Table 6.3 Visitors to Foundation RavennAntica museums, 2002–2017 (Fondazione RavennAntica)

Years	Domus	TAMO	Rasponi Crypt	Total
2002	7,708	-	-	7,708
2003	52,887	-	-	52,887
2004	59,648	47,000	-	106,648
2005	58,340	46,000	-	104,340
2006	57,651	53,000	-	110,651
2007	56,871	43,000	-	99,871
2008	54,593	47,244	-	101,837
2009	58,015	50,783	15,517	124,315
2010	56,624	40,479	20,600	117,703
2011	60,982	30,584	25,864	117,430
2012	45,089	33,540	17,543	96,172
2016	60,592	37775	25815	124,182
2017	72,565	42,075	29,081	143,721

Table 6.4 Visitors to and income generated by RavennAntica Foundation museums, 2010–2017 (Fondazione RavennAntica)

Year	Inputs	Income (€)		
	Total	Schoolchildren (within the total)	Ticket office	Bookshop
2010	117,703	9,638	188,859.00	56,552.62
2011	117,430	9,639	218,262.50	47,573.76
2012	96,172	11,871	210,159.50	49,505.44
2016	124,182	14,171	260,793.00	74,590.36
2017	143,721	15,913	342,717.00	81,162.76

In this framework, the RavennAntica recorded only one moment of stagnation, resulting from the transformation of the Complex of San Nicolò from a space dedicated to temporary exhibitions to the permanent location of the TAMO. However, the data referring to 2017 show more than 143,000 RavennAntica museum visits, generating revenue of approximately 430,000 euros.

Conclusion

The survey underpinning this chapter drew on the experiences of profoundly different museum organisations in terms of management and socioeconomic tourism and cultural context, providing extremely interesting insights regarding the contribution of each organisation to local economic development.

The Pinacoteca di Brera is the most established entity of the three analysed, to the extent that it is permanently included in the top 20 of the most visited cultural sites in Italy. What seems to have the greatest impact on the management of the Pinacoteca is not so much the *quantity* of tourist flows directed towards the city of Milan (which is one of the most visited cities not only in Italy, but also in Europe and the world), but rather their *quality*. Unlike Rome or Florence – cultural cities in which 'generalist' tourism prevails – in Milan, a large slice of the tourism is comprised by tourists who have already visited the city and have returned to experience it more deeply. Such tourists are 'intercepted' by the Pinacoteca, whose management is openly oriented towards high-quality cultural tourism, which generally coincides with return tourism. In fact, the Pinacoteca does not consider an increase in visitors a strategic objective; rather, it considers this a by-product of proper museum management, driven by the enhancement and protection of the cultural heritage in its collection for the benefit of the entire community. It should be stressed that, unlike generalist tourism – which is particularly vulnerable to exogenous shocks such as the terrorism risk or fluctuations in the exchange rate – return tourism is, by its very nature, richer and creates large positive externalities due to the greater spending capacity of returning tourists. Thus, the behaviour of returning tourism complements the socio-economic characteristics of Milan. As noted previously, the province of Milan registers a value added per inhabitant that is almost double the national average and a particularly low unemployment rate.

In contrast to the Pinacoteca, the MArTA suffers from a poor socio-economic context where it is located. Nonetheless, it is in the midst of a relaunch, and is capable of overcoming its challenges and pursuing new opportunities. Along with the atavistic problems that characterise southern Italian cities, Taranto adds the thorny problem of the ILVA reconversion, which has not only aggravated the local unemployment problems but also conveyed a negative image of the city, due to the steel plant's effect on the local environment and health. At the same time, Taranto exhibits a great potential, especially in terms of cultural tourism, which MArTA seems primed to take full advantage of. It emerges, therefore, that MArTA's management is very focused on tourism dynamics and seeks to transform the museum into a flywheel for local development. The management wants to regain the lost link with the community, open itself up to generalist tourism and abandon any traces of the self-referential proclivities that previously led it to lose contact with local residents. It is no coincidence, in fact, that one of its management results in recent years was precisely that of including the museum in the strategic plan for tourism in Apulia in order to enhance its tourist appeal. MArTA management also aims at increasing cooperation with local institutional, economic and business actors in order to develop tourist packages around specific cultural routes and to benefit from general tourism promotion. In this regard, it has built strong communication strategies on social media. MArTA aims at generating a positive socio-economic impact at local level by stimulating cultural tourism flows; to do so, it will use cultural conversion, following the model set by many European cities.

In a similar vein, even the RavennAntica Foundation – while characterised by a totally different governance model from the other two institutions and a different (dynamic) socio-economic context – seems keen to seize the opportunities of cultural tourism and deliver a positive local impact. On the other hand, one of its main objectives is precisely that of enhancing the archaeological, architectural and historical-artistic heritage of Ravenna also for tourist purposes. Achieving a combination of conservation, tourist enhancement and business management has, in fact, emerged as the mission of the foundation and may represent a significant opportunity for local development and the enrichment of Italy's cultural heritage.

Overall, therefore, the three cases analysed – the Pinacoteca di Brera, MArTA and the RavennAntica Foundation – highlight different ways to dealing with tourism and exploiting its potential in order to contribute to local economic development through induced flows of cultural tourism.

Notes

1 Parts of this chapter are a free reworking and interpretation of interviews conducted with Dr. James Bradburne (Director of the Pinacoteca di Brera, Dr. Eva Degl'Innocenti (Director of MArTA) and Prof. Giuseppe Sassatelli (President of the RavennAntica Foundation). The authors thank all of them for their valuable collaboration. In any case, the authors remain responsible for the contents reported here.

2 The Director of a museum with the qualification of executive office:

a) plans, directs, coordinates and monitors all museum management activities, including the organisation of exhibitions, as well as the study, enhancement, communication and promotion of museum heritage;

b) takes care of the museum's cultural project, making it a vital, inclusive place, capable of promoting the development of culture;

c) establishes the opening hours of the museum in order to ensure the widest possible enjoyment;

d) ensures high quality standards in management and communication, as well as educational and technological innovation;

e) ensures full cooperation with the Directorate General for Museums, the Regional Secretary, the Director of the Regional Museum Centre and Superintendents;

f) ensures a close relationship with the local stakeholders;

g) authorises the lending of cultural goods from its own collection (after consulting the relevant Directorates General and, in the case of loans abroad, the Directorate General for Museums);

h) authorises the study and publication of materials and directly (or by way of concession) awards activities and services

i) conducts public museum valorisation;

j) assists the Directorate General for Budget and the Directorate General for Museums in soliciting donations from private individuals in support of culture;

k) carries out research activities, the results of which are made public;

l) carries out the functions of a contracting station.

3 In this way, each type of user is able to benefit from a dedicated cultural offer, as in the case of children with workshops, the general public with thematic visits and the specialists with specific meetings. In addition, so-called 'MArTA Wednesdays' have been instated, offering free conferences and 'conversations at the museum', involving in-depth analyses of particular topics. In addition, a cultural and pedagogical programme has been implemented to ensure the function of the museum as a cultural mediator between its heritage and users, providing the keys to understanding and interpreting its own heritage assets.

4 The museum has become one of the top two most engaged Italian museums on social media. The MarTA Director has also interfaced with the Apulia Region and the Regional Tourism Agency (Pugliapromozione) in order to engage with regional communication circuits as well as national and international ones.

5 In this framework, it is worth mentioning the Interreg Italy-Greece, led by the University of Foggia.

6 The activation of new tourist routes, in addition to increasing the employment of many young graduates, has also significantly increased the average duration of visits to the city, with very positive effects on local commercial activities.

References

DPCM n° 171 del 29 agosto (2014) (Regolamento di organizzazione del Ministero dei beni e delle attività culturali e del turismo, degli uffici della diretta collaborazione del Ministro e dell'Organismo indipendente di valutazione della performance, a norma dell'articolo 16, comma 4, del D.L. n° 66 del 24 aprile 2014, convertito, con modificazioni, dalla L. n° 89 del 23 giugno 2014) (14G00183). GU Serie Generale n. 274 del 25-11-2014.

Destination Cities Index (2017) https://newsroom.mastercard.com/wp-content/uploads/2017/10/Mastercard-Destination-Cities-Index-Deck.pdf.

7 How a heritage asset as a tourist attraction can create regional value

Best practice from Europe and the United States

Introduction

The present chapter aims at describing a series of successful European and US cases in the management of heritage assets, particularly with regard to their ability to generate economic and social value for their local region.

The discussion begins with the case of the Guggenheim Museum in Bilbao – an extraordinary architectural and cultural operation that radically changed the face and economy of the Spanish city. Less well known than the Basque case is that of the Serralves Foundation, located in the nearby city of Porto, which has the goal of engaging in constant dialogue with the local city to create a support community. The third case study is that of the National Museums of Liverpool, a single institution that comprises eight museums, all with free entry, financed predominantly by the UK government but seeking new forms of livelihood. The chapter closes the slideshow of European cases with the Italian case of the Merano Thermal Baths, located in the region of the Autonomous Province of Bolzano, bridging the German-speaking world. Finally, the chapter concludes with a discussion of two US cases. The first is the case of Balboa Park in San Diego, California – a complex and articulated organisation comprising tens of museums, institutions and commercial activities; the second is the case of the Museum of Fine Arts in Boston, Massachusetts – the fifth largest museum complex in the United States, as well as one of the oldest.[1]

Guggenheim Museum in Bilbao

From an abandoned port to one of the most iconic museums in the world, the Guggenheim Museum in Bilbao emerged from the crisis that, in the late 1980s, effectively left a large section of the port area of Bilbao (along the Nervion River running through the city) deserted. The resulting decommissioned buildings in this area inspired the Solomon R. Guggenheim Foundation, in 1991, to imagine a new headquarters, modelled after their existing buildings in New York and Venice.

The Basque government proposed an agreement with the foundation, offering to fund the building, which was estimated to cost approximately $150 million. In return, the foundation agreed to manage the new institution and to use the building to organise temporary exhibitions, with some featuring works from the permanent collection of the American museum.

The project was entrusted to the architectural star Frank O. Gehry, who designed an external structure characterised by random curves, glass and titanium – designed to capture sunlight. The interior was designed around a large bright atrium overlooking the river and the surrounding landscape. Eleven thousand square meters of exhibition space were distributed over 19 galleries, of which 10 had the classic orthogonal shape while the remaining 9 irregularly shaped and could be identified from the outside by their organic forms and titanium coated vortexes. The largest tunnel measured 30 m in width and 130 m in length.

On 3 October 1997, the inauguration events began, culminating on 19 October with the public opening of the museum. In its first year, more than 1.3 million people visited the new institution – a number that tripled the expectations of the museum, itself, and comprised the first signs of what was later named the 'Bilbao effect'.[2] Accordingly, the city was totally rebranded from an industrial city in crisis to a tourist and cultural destination with an entirely new economic structure.

One of the aspects that makes the Guggenheim Museum in Bilbao a leading institution and interesting case study is its governance model, which combines public and private participation. Specifically, the governing body is divided into the following groups:

- 'patrons', comprised of representatives of the founders (i.e. the Basque government, the Provincial Council of Biscay (Bizkaia), the Solomon R. Guggenheim Foundation) and non-founding trustees; this group is presided over by the Lehendakari (i.e. President) of the Basque government;
- an executive committee comprised of two representatives of each of the founders, one from the city council of Bilbao and up to four representatives of non-founding trustees; this group is presided over by the President of the Province of Biscay; and
- a management team, headed by the Director General of the Museum, who is appointed by the Executive Committee.

The museum's management policy is oriented towards long-term sustainability and aims at balancing its income sources while also pursuing self-financing. The museum generates financial flows from three main sources: revenue generated by visitors, contributions from individual members and investment from public institutions. In 2017, public contributions to the museum's activities (from the Basque government, the Provincial Council of Biscay and the city of Bilbao) amounted to approximately 9 million euros.

In 2017, the museum's balance sheet, which closed with a pre-tax profit of 584,736 euros, recorded income from activities of 17,700,702 euros, of which: 11,280,000 came from grants, donations and legacies; 5,661,677 was contributed by the founders and supporters; and 759,025 stemmed from affiliations and association fees. Revenues from sales amounted to 10,392,626 euros, of which 9,091,004 were attributable to ticket sales. In 2017, the museum recorded 1,322,611 visitors, representing a 13% increase on the previous year. The museum's costs predominantly relate to external custody services (23,276,263 euros) and personnel (5,111,716 euros).

The museum has a clear price policy, with an entrance ticket price in line with that of other large exhibiting institutions (16 euros) and a concession price (9 euros) for students and pensioners. A particularly successful formula is reserved for 'Friends of the Museum', who pay an annual fee to the museum (ranging from 40 to 650 euros) in return for free entrance and the opportunity to participate in community events. In 2017, 27,500 people subscribed to this scheme. Similarly, the museum offers companies the opportunity to join the museum network. In 2017, 127 firms did so through sponsored initiatives, with the resulting benefits that they were able to use the museum for corporate events and communication, obtain free entrance for employees and customers and purchase corporate gifts at a generous discount.

The impact study conducted by B + I Strategy (most recent version 2017) demonstrates the ways in which the Guggenheim Museum in Bilbao has effectively contributed to and changed the face of Bilbao's economy.[3] Based on the concept of triple sustainability (or the triple effect), in addition to strictly economic effects (which remain at the centre of the analysis and are calculated in greater detail), the study considered the environmental and social, artistic and cultural impacts of the museum in its local context.

In line with the standard method for estimating economic impact, the study used the Leontief model, which distinguishes economic impacts as direct, indirect or induced by calculating two main orders of expenditure: internal (e.g. visitor expenditure on tickets, guided tours, food and bookstore purchases) and external (e.g. visitor expenditure on hotels, restaurants and transportation in the Basque territory) to the museum. The results were calculated with respect to Basque Country GDP,[4] employment and tax revenues.

To calculate the final value of the economic impact, three factors were considered:

- money spent by companies, institutions and individuals within the museum in the form of subscriptions, contributions, direct and indirect sponsorship and the purchase of tickets, merchandise and food (as recorded in the museum's balance sheet);
- expenses related to events organised inside the museum, such as conferences, book presentations, award ceremonies and workshops (as recorded in the museum's balance sheet); and

- money spent by visitors outside the museum for accommodation, transportation, entertainment, shopping and food (calculated on the basis of a market survey conducted with 3,219 tourists in December 2015 and March and August 2016).

With reference to the 2016 annularity, the B + I Strategy (2017) study calculated the overall economic impact of the museum on the territory to be approximately 485.3 million euros. Of this amount, 32.2 million (6.6%) was spent within the museum, while the remaining (453.1 million) was spent in the local area, largely in the hospitality sector. Furthermore, museum activities generated 424.6 million euros GDP and guaranteed 9,086 jobs. The Basque Country also benefited from higher tax revenues, to the value of 65.8 million euros, considering direct, indirect and induced effects.

Beyond generating these strictly economic effects, since its inauguration in 1997, the museum has become a regional tourist 'pole of attraction' and a main engine for the architectural and social transformation and revitalisation of the Basque capital. Reviewing the data on the participation of the Basque population in museum activities, we may also note the role played by the museum for local social and cultural development. It is estimated that, in 2016, more than 125,000 Basques (5% of the population) attended museum exhibitions and approximately 34,000 students, 8,700 families and 3,000 local individuals participated in the museum's socially oriented educational workshops (B + I Strategy, 2017). Finally, the international media impact that the Guggenheim generates for the region should not be overlooked.

In order to continue this development trajectory and maintain a prominent position among contemporary art institutions, the museum's management team aims at expanding the building structure; however, to date, this request has been opposed by the owning parties. An initial project of 'discontinuous expansion' – involving the construction of a secondary structure in the Biscay region of Urdaibai – began in 2008 but was subsequently suspended after the first phase, both because of the economic crisis and – especially – because of opposition from the Basque government.[5]

According to some critics (Vicario, 2017), the model of economic and tourist development in Bilbao that has been triggered by the Guggenheim is not sustainable in the long term, as the museum is detached from the local context. According to Vicario (2017), the Guggenheim in Bilbao is merely the 'franchise' of a multinational company; it is funded and owned by the Basque government, but controlled remotely, namely by the Guggenheim Foundation in New York. Vicario (2017), claims that the museum is a mere container – incapable of generating cultural production because it does not design the cultural bid itself, but follows the lead of the central offices in New York. He suggests that further investment in urban regeneration projects in Bilbao will be inherently unstable, as they will be based on tourism and commerce, and thus highly speculative. Furthermore, the employment patterns created in urban redevelopment projects tend to be highly polarised, characterised by a relatively low number of high paid managerial jobs and a much higher number of low paid low skilled jobs in the service sector. This latter condition could generate an unspecialised labour force, thereby impoverishing and condemning the social base of the region to subordination. However, this concern is shared by all tourist regions that arise from significant external investments.

Serralves Foundation, Porto

In the period immediately following the Carnations Revolution – which, in 1974, paved the way to democracy in Portugal – the city of Porto was the home to a series of movements seeking visibility for the numerous works of art produced during that intense and tumultuous period. In this context, many institutions, including the Center for Contemporary Art (active until 1980), tried to meet these demands, and the Portuguese government recognised such an authoritativeness in Porto that it selected the city as the home of a new National Museum of Contemporary Art.

The Serralves Villa and Park were chosen for the museum site. The villa had been constructed from 1925 to 1944 as a private residence for the second Count of Vizela, Carlos Alberto Cabral (1895–1968) and immediately consecrated as the best example of Art Deco in Portugal. The Republic of Portugal acquired the property in 1986 and opened the villa and park to the public in the following year.

The Museum of Contemporary Art, which was commissioned by the Serralves Foundation to the archivist Álvaro Siza in 1991, made Serralves, together with the historical nucleus, the auditorium and the library, one of the main cultural institutions of Portugal and a European centre of art and contemporary architecture.

The Serralves Foundation – dating to 1989 – was sanctioned by law (D. Lgs 240-A / 89, 27 July 1989) but represents the result of a process of bringing together public, private and civil society. The foundation has more than 50 original founders and 240 members. Among these are the Portuguese government, numerous municipalities, religious bodies, private citizens, national radio and television networks, TAP airlines, El Corte Inglés department stores, Boston Consulting Group, Ikea and JVC.[6]

The foundation's governing bodies, established by decree in 1989, include:

- the Council of Founders, who are tasked with setting the strategic directions; only Founders or institutions that have guaranteed 'services relevant to the Foundation' may sit on the Council of Founders, and all appointments – proposed by the Board of Directors – must be approved by the Board by an absolute majority;
- the Board of Directors, made up of nine members, including a Chairman/ Director and three deputies; each Director remains in office for three years and the new Director is selected by the Council of Founders, excluding

> two members appointed by the State, via a secret vote and absolute
> majority; and
> • the Executive Committee, comprised of the Director and two Vice-
>   Presidents, who are nominated by the Board of Directors and approved
>   via secret ballot and an absolute majority.

Since its establishment until the end of 2017, more than 9 million visitors have visited Serralves. Of these, more than 7 million have visited the complex since the museum opening in 1999. In 2017, the number of annual visitors rose to more than 834,300, showing an increase of 22% over the previous year and marking a new record. The number of foreign visitors has also grown significantly over recent years, exceeding 218,000 in 2017 (representing a 35% increase over the previous year). Furthermore, since the museum opened, it has provided educational programmes to more than 116,000 children and young people (Fundação de Serralves, 2017). In 2017, the Serralves Foundation recorded pre-tax revenue of 156,863,500 euros.

Each year, the Serralves Foundation publishes a detailed report of the impacts of its activities, drawing a picture of the previous year and outlining trajectories for the future, in a view to transparency and accountability. Da Silva Costa at Porto Business School (2013) estimated the direct, indirect and induced impacts of the Serralves Foundation on the local economy, also highlighting the link between the foundation and its various stakeholders (i.e. local and foreign visitors, cultural representatives, educators, industrial and commercial enterprises, public institutions and civil society) (Da Silva Costa, 2013). The objective of the study was to provide insights that could strengthen the Serralves Foundation's positioning as not only a cultural and creative institute and tourist attraction, but also a welcoming place for creative enterprise, a social accelerator and an economic agent capable of generating employment, consumption and profit for the entire region.

In carrying out its economic assessment of the Serralves Foundation, the study considered all primary and secondary effects, using measures such as production, added value, family income, employment and tax revenue. The direct impact of the foundation's artistic and cultural activity was quantified using information on the management fees related to its service provision. The expenditure for the foundation's artistic and cultural services was calculated on the basis of its accounting data. Finally, itinerant exposure was measured using the transfers paid to the Serralves Foundation, as well as an estimate of the expenses incurred by the organising bodies.

Using input-output analysis, the study estimated (using the Leontief method) indirect effects associated with inter-industrial exchanges and the household consumption of workers who were directly and indirectly employed by the Serralves Foundation. The artistic-cultural compound was analysed according to three categories of enterprises. The first consisted of the Serralves Foundation, the Serralves Restaurant, the Serralves Bookstore, the Serralves Store and other incubated companies in the foundation. The second category included institutions that collaborated with Serralves, while not providing services to Serralves. Finally, the third category included parties that benefited from the existence of Serralves but whose effect could not be measured via intermediate consumption. This latter group included institutions involved in accommodation, transportation, catering and trade, which provided complementary services outside the artistic-cultural area, fuelling the induced circuit.

Evaluation of the third category required an estimation of the tourist flows that could be attributed to Serralves; accordingly, the research involved sample surveys, which the authors administered to tourists in the city of Porto. From their analysis, it emerged that the Serralves Foundation had a significant impact as a public educator, a provider of public services and social inclusion and a multiplier of quality of life in the city.

Following the methodology described above, the study, which took as reference the year 2010, estimated that the activity of the Serralves Foundation artistic-cultural compound contributed approximately 40.6 million euros to the GDP, created 1,296 jobs (full-time equivalent) and generated approximately 20.7 million euros in fees and 10.7 million in tax revenue. It also estimated that the foundation's activities, together with visitors' expenditure, triggered multiplier effects amounting to approximately 3.4 million euros contributed to the GDP via employment, approximately 3.5 million euros for salaries and 3.3 million euros for tax revenue at the regional level.

As regards the type of visitor to the Serralves Foundation artistic-cultural compound, the results of the survey showed that the site was particularly attractive to young and skilled persons with a strong preference for cultural activities and the environment. It is this aspect that makes Serralves a unique case in the panorama of contemporary art museums.

National Museums Liverpool

Eight museums, more than 3 million visitors per year, an estimated economic impact of approximately 53 million pounds and an impact on social welfare that potentially reaches up to 130 million pounds. All of this describes National Museums Liverpool (NML), one of the most important museum groups in the world as well as the only English public museum network located outside of London (i.e. Liverpool, a UNESCO World Heritage city and 2008 European Capital of Culture).

Born as a museum network in 1986, when the government decided to create a national trust for museum management, the 'National Museums and Galleries on Merseyside', which became 'National Museums Liverpool' in 2003, is financed by the British government (contributing two-thirds of the financial capital) through the Department for Digital, Culture, Media & Sport, as well as by its own revenues (amounting to one-third of its financial capital).[7]

NML is governed by a Board of Directors comprised of 14 to 20 members, all appointed by the UK government. The Board of Directors appoints a Director and ratifies the appointment of the executive team, which is composed of five directors for the following functional areas: visitors and educational programmes, human resources, sales and marketing, finance and development.

The NML museums include the International Slavery Museum, which is the only museum in the world dedicated to slavery; the Lady Lever Art Gallery, which boasts one of the most beautiful decorative art collections in the United Kingdom; the Merseyside Maritime Museum, which symbolises the revitalisation of Liverpool's iconic waterfront area; the Walker Art Gallery, one of the most beautiful European art galleries, with masterpieces by Rembrandt and Monet and collections of Victorian and pre-Raphaelite art; the World Museum, which was inaugurated in 1853 and therefore the oldest of all museums, with a collection that spans millions of years; Sudley House, which is a stately home located in the southern outskirts of Liverpool housing the exclusive collection of the Victorian merchant George Holt, with antique furniture and paintings by Turner; the Border Force National Museum, which is dedicated to customs officers; and the Liverpool Museum, which is the flagship NML museum and has been visited by more than 5 million people. In 2013, the Liverpool Museum won an award from the Council of Europe for its demonstrated ability to promote human rights and community spirit, tracing the history of the city of Liverpool – one of the most controversial in Great Britain.

While all of the individual museums are part of a single legal entity – NML – they each have their own director, who reports to the Directorate General. NML's 2017/2018 fiscal year (running from 1 April 2017 to 31 March 2018) closed with an operating income of more than 20 million pounds, generally due to a revaluation of assets. In detail, NML recorded revenues of 28.612 million pounds, costs of 32.348 million and a positive balance from the revaluation of assets, amounting to 23,789 million (National Museums Liverpool, 2018).

As regards the composition of the revenues, approximately two-thirds (19.761 million pounds) derived from transfers by the British government through the DCMS, while another 1.996 million came from the Heritage Lottery Fund, which distributes the proceeds of national lotteries. Furthermore, the NML directly contributed 4.248 million to the budget via revenue earned from commercial activities (mainly museum cafes and bookshops), and received direct collections to the value of 2.242 million.

With 1.5 million inhabitants and an economy worth 28 billion pounds (largely tied to the port and sea industries), the city of Liverpool, following great economic difficulties in the 1970s and 1980s, has shown tremendous economic growth, although the regional GDP is still 25% lower than the UK average and the 34 neighbouring areas are among the 100 most disadvantaged in England. The region's economic disadvantage affects the health, well-being and education of local residents, who present a lower life expectancy and worse educational outcomes than the national average; further, a quarter of its youth live in poverty. This situation became particularly critical in the years of the economic crisis, due to cuts in public spending (since 2010, the health budget, alone, has been reduced by 15%). In this context, culture has played a strategic role in revitalising the region. In fact, the regional supply of cultural assets has placed Liverpool at the centre of a new model of tourism development, making it the fifth most visited city in the United Kingdom, with approximately 56 million visitors each year. This result was also achieved thanks to the extraordinary offer of NML museums, which independently attract an average of 3 million visitors each year (with a record high of 3,305,671 visitors in 2017).

In order to gain insight into the impact generated by NML on the local economy and society, we can consider the report from Regeneris Consulting (2017), which highlights that NML visitors have grown 360% since 2000. The report shows that 40% of tourists to Liverpool visit an NML museum, and 67% of residents visit an NML museum more than once a year – and in fact, almost once a month –a testament to the very close relationship between the museums and the city. In fact, one of the main characteristics of the NML museum system is its inclusiveness.

The NML model ensures that the museums are open and accessible to everyone. It is not surprising, therefore, that 27% of the visitors are pensioners and that visits from persons in disadvantaged socio-economic groups (28%) are much greater than those recorded by other national museums. While all NML museums offer free entry, it is possible to purchase a membership and, in so doing, acquire various benefits, such as discounts in bars, restaurants and shops in the museum network, invitations to special events, periodic newsletters and dedicated guides. There are several types of membership on offer: annual membership ranges from 30 to 75 pounds (for two adults and three children), while permanent membership can cost up to 1,000 pounds; and with an even greater economic commitment (between 1,000 and 5,000 pounds each year), one can become an NML 'Patron'.

As highlighted by Regeneris Consulting (2017), in the last year surveyed, NML generated of 1,210 jobs, of which 550 had a direct, indirect or induced effect in the city of Liverpool; furthermore, the total annual impact of NML on GDP in the entire northwest of England was an estimated 53 million pounds.

Over the same period, the museum purchased more than 10 million pounds worth of goods from UK-based suppliers, of which more than 3 million pounds was attributable to suppliers in the city of Liverpool and 5.5 million was attributable to suppliers in the northwest. In addition, the flow of visitors from outside the city of Liverpool (1.5 million people in 2015/16) spent approximately 34 million pounds in their time spent in Liverpool – in hotels, bars, restaurants and shops. Of this 34 million, at least 6 million was spent by foreign tourists.

From a social point of view, NML has become a reference point for more than 400 educational institutions; it enjoys many collaborations with British and international universities and collaborates on two postgraduate courses (i.e. Museum and Heritage Studies; Art History and Curating) at Liverpool Hope University. Furthermore, in an effort to give voice to the local community, NML runs volunteer projects that, to date, have involved more than 160 people (including many elderly persons) and has signed partnerships with charitable organisations such as the Prince's Trust, the Anthony Walker Foundation and Wicked Fish. NML also leads the Federation of International Human Rights Museums, born out of the work of the International Slavery Museum and established in 2010 under the aegis of UNESCO, and in 2014 led the promotion of the Alliance for Social Justice for Museums. Finally, NML also launched the 'Happy Older People' network, aimed at involving older people in artistic activities (currently more than 2,700 participants) and the National Alliance for Museums, Health & Wellbeing, which shares information on museums and health, contributing to the creation of new best practice.

In pursuing its strategy of social inclusiveness – not only for the city of Liverpool but also for the entire northwest of England – NML has improved the living conditions of vulnerable people and given voice to those on the margins of society. In order to continue on this path, NML aims at expanding its exhibitions and thematic initiatives, renovating its buildings, improving visits and strengthening the 'House of Memories' – an initiative dedicated to the treatment of senile dementia that, in 2017, celebrated its fifth anniversary through the launch of a new wellness programme for older people and their chaperones. NML will also continue to increase its online presence. In 2017, alone, the NML website recorded a 44% increase in traffic over the previous year and generated 21,933 new subscribers to its YouTube channel, which had – by the end of that year – amassed more than 4 million views. In the same year, NML had 109,380 followers on Twitter, 90,838 fans on Facebook and 12,179 followers on its 22 Instagram accounts associated with individual museums in its network.

Merano Thermal Baths

The history of the Merano Thermal Baths is closely linked to that of the city of Merano – the capital of Burgraviato.[8] Already in the 1520s, the emperor Charles V demonstrated an appreciation of the particular microclimate of this territory and willingly made a stopover in Merano when he moved to the area. Merano's moniker as the 'city of care' was bestowed in 1836, when the physician Josef Waibl published a study on the advantages of Merano's mild climate. In a short time, the city became famous as one of the most important climatic areas in Europe, and nobles and artists from all over the world spent more or less long stays in the small town along the Passirio. In particular, characters such as Richard Strauss, Rainer Maria Rilke, Franz Kafka and even Princess Sissi with her daughter benefited from Merano's fresh air and good water.

Starting in the 1840s, nursing homes began to open and this new activity encouraged the construction of villas and large hotels. In 1874, the famous 'Kurhaus' of Merano was inaugurated; this institution offered treatments involving grapes, steam baths, radioactive water and much more. From this moment on, the city's tourist history truly began.

After a period of stagnation during the First World War, Merano's economy – strongly linked to health and well-being – was stimulated in 1933 when a geologist discovered water containing radon on Mount San Vigilio. Thanks to this new resource, the already famous health resort became a spa resort.

In 1972, the Società Azionaria Lavorazione Valorizzazione Acque Radioattive (SALVAR) (founded in 1958) opened the Merano Thermal Baths, fed by the springs of Mount San Vigilio. The therapeutic applications included mud baths, whirlpools, inhalations and hydroponic treatments, as well as baths in a large indoor pool. In 1982, the company changed its name from SALVAR to Meraner Kurbad AG – Terme Merano. At that time, the Italian state was the majority shareholder, with 60% equity.

At the end of 1997, the Autonomous Province of Bolzano, already in possession of 39% of the shares, became the majority shareholder, marking the beginning of a new era of the Merano Thermal Baths, which today have the legal form of a joint stock company, with 99.8% owned by the Autonomous Province of Bolzano and 0.2% owned by the Municipality of Merano and the Merano Care and Residence Company.

The province's decision to invest in this company derived from its desire to completely revive the thermal establishment in order to increase Meranese tourism. To this end, it organised a design competition involving 112 architects from all over Europe. On 12 January 2000, the winners were chosen – Berlin-based structural architects Rüdiger Baumann and Julia Zillich and Berlin-based landscape architects Cornelia Müller and Jan Wehberg of Lützow. For the realisation of the interiors, the famous Milanese designer – of Altoatesina origin – Matteo Thun was chosen. Work started in autumn 2001. On 3 December 2005, the Merano Thermal Baths were inaugurated and, on 3 June 2006, the Merano Thermal Park opened to the public. The large hotel that completed the bath complex – originally a provincial property – was sold, after a series of management challenges, to a group of private investors led by the Ebner Group, southern Tyrol's main publisher with extensive interests in real estate and tourism.

As regards the investments in the new compound, critical issues were not lacking. The renewal project, which started in 1999, had a budget of 79.5 million euros but a total expenditure of 122 million. The spa compound cost 62 million euros (compared with the budgeted 38 million), the new hotel cost 41.5 million euros (compared to the budgeted 19 million), the underground garage cost 14.5 euros (compared to the budgeted 11.3 million) and the via Terme basement (paid for by the Municipality of Merano) cost 9 million euros (compared to the budgeted 7.7 million). A further 8.6 million euros was spent on drilling in search of new hot springs (Rossi, 2014).

To cope with the costs of construction and, subsequently, budgetary losses, the province agreed to a long series of capital investments. In 1999, it paid 2.5 million euros towards design costs; in 2000, it paid 1.9 million towards the same costs and, in the period 2001–2005, it paid 7.8 million each year. In 2004, the province made a capital contribution of 9.1 million euros. In 2005, 5.85 million euros was paid towards drilling and, in the period 2006–2009, a further 4 million per year were paid for the same purpose. The 2013–2015 plan for the Merano Thermal Baths provided for further payments by the province of 18 million euros, both for the service contract and for capital increases, while the current service contract, agreed in 2016, provides for provincial contributions of approximately 2.8 million euros per year.

Terme Merano is governed by a Board of Directors comprised of five directors: in addition to the Chairman Andreas Cappello (in office since 2007) and the Deputy Chairman Sandra Lando, the directors include Irene Pechlaner (Director of the Merano Health District), Hansjörg Prast (Director of IDM Südtirol Alto Adige, the regional promotion company controlled by the province) and Alfred Strohmer (representative of Merano hoteliers).

Analysing the 2017 annual financial statements, particularly with respect to revenues from sales and services, we can note that the direct contributions of the Autonomous Province of Bolzano were fundamental in enabling the company to achieve profit. The service contract with the Autonomous Province of Bolzano agreed on 14 October 2014 refers to:

> the relationship between the company Terme Merano [which, we recall, is 99% owned by the Autonomous Province of Bolzano] and the Province, with regard to the exercise of the functions provided by the bylaws, of those delegated and/or entrusted, aimed at achieving the corporate purpose.

As a result of the contract, the Autonomous Province of Bolzano is called to 'implement the Terme Merano company in the context of the corporate purpose to carry out projects and concepts, develop and implement new offers and products, as well as the continuous improvement of the same' and to support this activity through an annual fee to Terme Merano of 3.5 million euros (IVA included). The contract was subsequently renewed to the end of 2018.

With regard to visitors to the Merano Thermal Baths, in 2015–2017 annual visitors exceeded 400,000 in each year. In 2017, the bath and sauna department, alone, registered 407,082 admissions, with an average of 1,115 per day. At the Spa & Vital Centre, 17,990 treatments were performed, including 8,277 massages (approximately 23 per day) and 1,736 baths (approximately five per day). The inhalation department showed greater use in the spring and autumn seasons but recorded 18,819 annual treatments.

Access to the spa complex is granted via a ticket that is differentiated according to the duration of the visit and the use of the thermal or sauna area. The price varies from 9 euros (for children, granting two hours of access on a weekday) to 27 euros (for adults seeking to use the complex for an entire day). There are also numerous packages providing special discounts, as well as a series of 'value cards' that can be purchased in 85-, 100-, 150- and 200-euro denominations and provide a 15% discount. The value cards are transferable (i.e. they can be used by more than one person and are valid only for entry to the spa and saunas). It should be noted that these cards are among the most popular items in the Merano Thermal Bath online shop: in 2017, 4,457 such coupons were purchased in the spa complex e-shop for a total revenue of 374,324 euros. This result has undoubtedly been supported by the Merano Thermal Baths' effective management of its online presence: in 2017, its online communication generated 468,195 unique website views with nearly three million pages consulted.

The company invests a significant amount in communication and marketing. In 2017, 80 journalists visited the spa, generating a series of positive reviews in media outlets including: *Gioia, Starbene, Vanity Fair, Bell'Italia, La Repubblica, La Stampa, La Freccia Collection, Panorama, GEO, Spiegel, NZZ, Für Sie, Blick, Die Freundin, Migrosmagazin* and *Münchner Merkur*.

In October 2015, Terme Merano released to the public a study on the economic impact of its activities (Schneider and Dreer, 2015), conducted by the economist and academic Friedrich Schneider of the Johannes Kepler Universität in Linz. The study, which referred to the company's first nine years of full operation (2006–2014), demonstrated that the activities of the Merano Thermal Baths had generated 302.7 million euros of added value through its employees' personal consumption, its revenues from operating the baths and the expenditure of its guests.

Balboa Park, San Diego

San Diego's Balboa Park is one of the world's most renowned public parks, spread over 1,200 acres (just under 490 hectares) and comprising enchanting gardens, dozens of attractions, a world-famous zoo and 17 museums.[9] Each year, it attracts more than 4.5 million visitors. Balboa Park is owned by the city of San Diego, which manages the park through its Department of Parks and Recreation. Management of the park is complex, since, on the one hand, the museums and attractions enjoy independent management and, on the other hand, the park as a whole is managed by two bodies: the aforementioned Department of Parks and Recreation and the Balboa Park Committee – a governing body appointed by the Mayor of San Diego and ratified by the San Diego City Council. An indeterminate number of non-profit organisations helps to support the park's activities: among these, the biggest are the Friends of Balboa Park and the 'Committee of 100', which was founded in 1967 to oppose the apportionment of part of the park and, following this, has been active in preserving the park's integrity (Balboa Park Committee, 2008, p. 5).

The lack of a clear administrative identity and the need for greater coordination among the dozens of organisations operating in its context are some of the most evident critical issues in Balboa Park's everyday management. The city of San Diego does not seem able to autonomously provide for Balboa Park's economic needs and the Balboa Park Committee thus serves to forge public-private partnerships to assist in the ordinary and extraordinary management of the park.

Crossed by several highways and two canyons (Cabrillo Canyon and Florida Canyon), Balboa Park is nestled in sunny San Diego – the eighth largest city in the United States and the second largest city in California, with 1.4 million inhabitants. More than 30% of resident households have an annual household income of more than $100,000 and the county has one of the highest percentages of residents with a university or advanced education degree. With its dynamic artistic and cultural aspects, Balboa Park has been an integral part of the city's culture for more than a century. Between August 2016 and August 2017, in particular, 4,681,922 people visited the park, including 2,635,922 local residents and 2,046,000 tourists. According to estimates by Testa et al. (2017), local residents access Balboa Park approximately 10 times a year, for a total of 28,405,222 visits. Among tourists, 19% report that Balboa Park was their main reason for visiting San Diego. Also as regards tourists, 78% stay in a hotel over a total of 311,650 annual nights, with an average stay of three nights at an average daily rate of $165.27 for approximately 2.4 people per room.

While access to the outdoor areas of the park is free – except when special events are running – each museum has a different pricing policy, but most extend free admission to local residents on one day of the week, as well as on special occasions such as Valentine's Day or Thanksgiving. Residents can also purchase subscriptions to Balboa Park, earning them the right to not only visit the museums and attractions for free, but also to access the backstage areas of special events.

In addition to its strong iconic value, Balboa Park has a significant impact on San Diego's economy. In particular, the Balboa Park Conservancy (2017) reported that the park has an overall economic impact on San Diego of approximately $356.4 million a year, of which 192 million is a direct effect.

In terms of taxation, the park generates $6.7 million through hotel taxes and $3.2 million through local taxes. Furthermore, park employment generates $52.9 million a year, dispersed between more than 14,000 full-time and part-time employees (the park also enjoys more than 26,000 volunteers). Most of the park's employees contribute to the museums and park events.

The park's impact on the real estate market is also extremely significant, and it is estimated that the value of the properties adjacent to Balboa Park has grown considerably over recent years, generating additional tax revenues for the municipality. Specifically, the impact assessment estimates a total of $92.5 million in value generated by both the increase in property values and the higher tax revenues (Testa et al., 2017).

Balboa Park also generates health, environmental and social benefits. For more than 40,000 persons, the park is a primary venue for engaging in physical activities and sport. Furthermore, the US Department of Forestry estimates that the park generates the equivalent of $390,695 per year in its positive impact on the environment via the carbon dioxide and rainwater absorbed by its vegetation.

As regards social impacts, in San Diego County, there is a high rate of juvenile crime; similar to other parts of the United States, in San Diego, the juvenile offense rate is closely linked to the limited presence of parents at home, often due to work. In recent years, however, the arrests of minors have decreased, and one contributing factor in this has been the educational and recreational programmes organised by Balboa Park, including summer camps and weekend workshops dedicated to art, music, dance and even Japanese culture, thanks to the Japanese Friendship Garden. In total, Balboa Park offers more than 250 opportunities through more than 100 recreational programmes in which 396,000 children and young people participate every year.

In 2018, Balboa Park celebrated its 150th anniversary. For the occasion, its structures were the subject of numerous renovations and significant redevelopment. Ongoing maintenance initiatives will align with the park's strategic objectives and further strengthen its green soul; one such initiative involves planting 500 new trees (with the support of public funds to the value of $378,000). Finally, the Balboa Park strategy aims at developing further partnerships and initiatives to encourage greater integration within the local community.

Museum of Fine Arts, Boston

With approximately 500,000 works on display, the Museum of Fine Arts (MFA) in Boston is one of the most famous and complete art museums in the world, as well as the fifth largest in the United States, attracting, on average, one million visitors each year. In 2017, it was visited by 1.192 million people, while almost 5 million browsed its website and 165,000 participated in its educational programmes.

Inaugurated on 4 July 1876, the museum was initially housed in Copley Square, with a collection of 5,600 works of art. But a sudden growth in the collection and visitors in 1909 led the museum to move to a new building overlooking Huntington Avenue, close to the prestigious School of Fine Arts (also founded in 1876). It has remained in that building ever since.

The museum's organisational and managerial autonomy dates back to 4 February 1870, when the Massachusetts Parliament promoted an act to establish

> a body corporate by the name of the Trustees of the Museum of Fine Arts for the purpose of erecting a museum for the preservation and exhibition of works of art, of making, maintaining, and exhibiting collections of such works, and of affording instruction in the Fine Arts.

Today, the museum is guided by a Board of Directors made up of 10 members and a much larger supervisory board – with a mainly consultative function – which counts over 100 members.

The museum's financial statements for 2017 showed an operating profit of $1.099 million, operating costs of $83.77 million, and revenues of $84.869 million.

The halls of the museum house its rich collection, which spans many cultures and historical periods. The artworks include Egyptian sarcophagi of immense artistic value; masterpieces of French impressionists and post-impressionists, including Gauguin, Renoir, Monet, Van Gogh and Cézanne; American art from the 18th and 19th centuries, by John Singleton Copley, Winslow Homer and John Singer Sargent; Chinese paintings, including some of the most precious in the history of the Empire; ancient codes, for which the MFA has the largest permanent exhibition space in the United States; and the largest collection of Japanese artworks outside Japan, including Edward S. Morse's collection of more than 5,000 ceramics. The MFA also hosts a very large exhibition of Korean art, four floors dedicated to art of the Americas and a gallery of contemporary art, in which more than 1,500 works have been exhibited between 1955 and today. In addition, the museum hosts one of the largest online art catalogues in the world, with more than 346,000 objects surveyed; screens approximately 500 films each year, attracting 35,000 film buffs; puts on 50 concerts, drawing more than 6,000 spectators; and organises 40 courses, in which 23,000 people participate.

Boston, a city with more than 600,000 inhabitants, is the capital of Massachusetts – the 12th richest state in the United States. It is considered the cultural and historical centre of New England and one of the world's major hubs for education, biotechnology, finance and architecture. In particular, Boston's cultural sector is highly developed, also thanks to the presence of more than 40 internationally renowned colleges and universities, including Harvard, MIT, Boston College, Boston University and Northeastern University. It is no wonder, then, that more than 1 million people visit the MFA on average each year, and 450,000 visitors arrive in Boston for precisely this reason. Among the latter, 50% are from Massachusetts, 22% are from another US state and 11% have an international passport. But in addition to hosting visitors, the MFA also works with companies to organise events and conventions.

The museum is open seven days a week, from 10 am to 5 pm, with two prolonged openings on Wednesdays and Fridays, from 10 am to 10 pm. Guided tours are available on each day, with multimedia formats and simultaneous translations in Chinese, French, German, Italian, Japanese, Portuguese, Russian and Spanish. Many of the exhibits are also accessible to blind and deaf visitors thanks to the use of special technological devices. Admission costs $25 for adults, $23 for students and pensioners and $10 for children aged 7 to 17 years; however, on some occasions (e.g. school holidays), children can access the museum for free. Free access is also extended to all children aged 0 to 6 years, as well as to Members or 'University Members'.

The museum offers various levels of annual membership (from the base 'Supporter' level at $75 to the 'Leader' at $2,999 and, at the highest end, 'Chairman's Circle Patron' at $100,000). Young adults can also purchase membership to the 'Museum Council' (ranging in price from $300 to 3,000 per year) – a group dedicated to benefactors aged 21 to 49 years interested in exclusive invitations to parties and 'meet ups' about art. 'University Membership', on the other hand, is reserved for students and faculty members of universities and colleges in Massachusetts, New Hampshire and Maine, and it provides discounts and a 'Guest Member Day', on which the University Members (along with their friends and relatives) can enjoy free admission. The museum also provides other special facilities for residents of Massachusetts; for the military and their family; for members of certain programmes (e.g. the Bank of America's Museums Programme); for teachers in Massachusetts, Connecticut, Maine, New Hampshire, Rhode Island and Vermont; and for students and staff of colleges across the Commonwealth. In addition, every Wednesday after 4 pm and on the occasion of five annual open days, admission to the museum is completely free for everyone. This initiative has encouraged the participation of more than 35,000 persons who would otherwise never have planned a visit. The MFA facilities are supported by the Massachusetts Cultural Council – a state agency that values the cultural life of Massachusetts communities.

It is evident, therefore, that the MFA is an extraordinary cultural, educational and economic resource for the local region. A study by the Economic Development Research Group (2015) (Economic Development Research Group, 2015) showed that, in 2014, the MFA generated a total economic impact of $338 million in Boston and $409 million in Massachusetts. As regards the city of Boston, $143 million was generated directly by museum expenses, including staff salaries, restaurant services, cleaning and parking, costs associated with the School of Fine Arts and costs associated with suppliers. Equally relevant was the economic driver generated by MFA visitors and students of the School of Fine Arts, equivalent to approximately $180 million. The study estimated, in fact, that the average daily spending of local (i.e. in-state) visitors was $64, while it was $389 for out-of-state tourists and $411 for international travelers.

As regards employment, the MFA is one of the largest employers in Boston, with 1,313 direct employees– of whom 565 are based in Boston and paid a total of approximately $23 million in annual salaries. Indirectly, the museum supports a further 3,441 jobs in Boston and 3,872 in Massachusetts. These are jobs created as a result of the expenditure of museum employees and visitors in hotels, restaurants and other services. To this can be added the approximately $500 million invested by the museum over the period 2004–2014 in construction, which contributed to the direct, indirect and induced creation of 3,397 jobs in Boston and 5,018 in Massachusetts. The number of jobs created by the MFA peaked during the 2008 economic depression, providing an important contribution to the community.

Each year, the MFA spends approximately $60 million on goods and services, with 25% of the suppliers based in Boston. As regards the hospitality sector, it is estimated that the million people who visit the museum each year spend approximately $168 million. Added to this, $11 million are spent by students of the School of Fine Arts and those who arrive in Boston to visit them.

Also important is the MFA's commitment to breaking down social barriers and improving livelihoods in the local community. To this end, the museum promotes activities such as the Community Arts Initiative – an afterschool programme with educational and recreational activities – and the Artful Healing programme – art workshops for patients in local hospitals. The MFA also engages in partnerships with many Boston communities, such as the Boston Chinatown Neighborhood Center, VietAID, the Chinese Cultural Connection in Malden and the Korean Cultural Society.

Great attention is also given to enhancing the artistic talent of young people through the School of Fine Arts. In partnership with the school, the MFA provides many activities and programmes for teachers, including an online MFA for Educators programme that enables teachers from around the world to create customised art lessons. Currently, the programme involves almost 4,000 participants, and it will be further strengthened in the coming years. In fact, in 2020, the MFA will celebrate its 150th anniversary, and it expects this event to coincide with an increasingly central role for the museum in the national and international artistic scene. It will pursue this objective by developing new partnerships and exhibitions, attracting more visitors and artists, enhancing its technological infrastructure, improving the visitor experience and expanding the gallery space dedicated to modern and contemporary art.

In a document entitled *MFA 2020*, published in 2017, a task force of 20 executives, board members, employees and consultants of the museum outlined the MFA's main critical issues. Subsequently, they set out a series of objectives to overcome these challenges. The document opens with five 'promises for the future': 'collect purposefully, collaborate generously, invite boldly, welcome warmly, engage deeply' (Museum of Fine Arts, 2017, p. 1). Through these promises, the authors identified a primary focus of expanding their visitor base: 'While we are committed to building and make more deep the relationship with the current audiences we also know that our future plan cannot succeed without a commitment to broaden our reach'. In particular, the MFA aims at growing three target segments: university students in Boston, for whom they imagine dedicated programmes capable of 'transforming them into life ambassadors' of the museum; families, especially those in Boston suburbs, who have been historically less connected to the museum; and professionals in cultural and creative industries, including artists, designers, architects, musicians, performers, writers, directors, multimedia producers and marketing and advertising professionals, who could become part of a specialised community and, again, function as ambassadors of the museum.

Having defined the frame of reference, the authors listed six critical issues on which to work to develop the museum into the future:

- improving the conservation of works in the collection and building new relationships with collectors (in order to increase – mainly through donations – the acquisition of new works), particularly with respect to twentieth- and twenty-first-century art;
- redesigning the entrance and all service areas, with the aim of making it less difficult for guests to understand the visiting paths and to provide a greater feeling of comfort and hospitality;
- offering more opportunities for contact with the local community (e.g. through dedicated visits or specific exhibitions) and simultaneously strengthening the MFA's international positioning by creating 'memorable content' to 'increase the reputation of the Museum as a thought leader';
- repositioning the MFA brand, redefining its key values in order to better 'build communities, involve new audiences and generate visitor flows';
- identifying new 'performance measurement tools to define expectations and achieve strategic objectives' and building a new organisational culture based on a wider sharing of objectives and a rigourous system for measuring results; and
- adopting 'a global financial strategy that faces the current and future well-being of the Museum, investing in the collection of quality data to support decision-making and improving the technological infrastructure for proactively anticipate and guarantee support through the strategic plan'.

Notes

1 The authors would like to thank Domenico Lanzilotta and BLUM for their precious help with the document analysis of the heritage assets detailed in this chapter. The authors take full responsibility for the content of the chapter.
2 Among the first to use this definition was Beatriz Plaza of the Faculty of Economics of the University of the Basque Country. See Plaza, B. (1999), The Guggenheim-Bilbao Museum effect: A reply to María V. Gomez's 'Reflective images: The case of urban regeneration in Glasgow and Bilbao'. *International Journal of Urban and Regional Research.* 23(3), 589–592.
3 B + I STRATEGY, (2017). *Estudio del impacto económico generado por la actividad of the Guggenheim Museum Bilbao 31 de Diciembre 2016.* The first edition of this study dates back to 2011.
4 'Basque Country', here, refers to the Basque Autonomous Community (Basque: 'Euskadi', Spanish: 'País Vasco'), and should not be confused with the geographical region inhabited by the Basque people in the region of the Pyrenees, including areas of France.

5 'The need for additional space to complement those existing in the museum remains a problem that must be addressed in the future with the Urdabiai solution or another, but it is a problem that must be solved', said Museum Director Juan Ignacio Vidarte, also highlighting the need to restart a campaign to acquire new works in the short term. For Vidarte, the museum collection, which currently boasts 130 works by 64 international artists, costing 110 million euros invested between 1996 and 2011 and currently valued at 770 million euros, is the 'backbone of the Museum and its best guarantee for the future'. See Unknown author (2016). Vidarte alerta de que el Guggenheim necesita más espacio expositivo y dice que Urdaibai 'sigue vigente'. *El Mundo*. 6 May.

6 The complete list of founders, constantly updated, can be found on the Foundation's website: www.serralves.pt.

7 The Department for Culture, Media & Sport (DCMS) also provides funding for the British Museum, the Imperial War Museums, the National Gallery, the Royal Museums of Greenwich, the Science Museum Group, the National Portrait Gallery, the Natural History Museum, the Royal Armories, Sir John Soane's Museum, the Tate, the Victoria and Albert Museum and the Wallace Collection. In 2017, the DCMS supported the United Kingdom's museum and gallery activities through contributions amounting to 443 million pounds. Recipients of the funding also included, *inter alia*, the BBC (3.267 billion pounds); the arts, culture and libraries sector (757 million pounds); and sport (463 million pounds). Department for Culture, Media and Sport, (2017). *Annual report and accounts 2016–17*. Department for Culture, Media and Sport, p. 15.

8 Burgraviato ('Burggrafenamt' in German, 'Burgraviat' in Latin) is the area around Merano in Alto Adige, as well as the name of the district with the capital of Merano. The name derives from the Burggraf of Tirolo County (i.e. the *burgravio* of the Tyrolean count). The Italian form of the name is derived from the phonetic adaptation of the original German term. The district includes the Val Passiria, the Val d'Ultimo, the Alta Val di Non and the Merano area of the Val d'Adige. The district is bordered on the west with Val Venosta, on the south with Oltradige-Bassa Atesina, on the northeast with Alta Valle Isarco and on the southeast with Salto-Sciliar (on the Salto plateau).

9 The 17 Balboa Park Museums include: the Fleet Science Center, Marston House, the Mingei International Museum, the Museum of Photographic Arts, the San Diego Air and Space Museum, the San Diego Art Institute, the San Diego Automotive Museum, the San Diego History Center, the San Diego Mineral and Gem Society, the San Diego Model Railroad Museum, the San Diego Museum of Man, the San Diego Natural History Museum, the San Diego Museum of Art, the Timken Museum of Art, the Veterans Museum at Balboa Park, the WorldBeat Center and the recently founded Comic-Con Museum.

References

Balboa Park Committee (2008), *The Future of Balboa Park*.

B + I Strategy (2017), *Estudio del Impacto Económico generado por la actividad del Museo Guggenheim Bilbao, 31 de Diciembre 2016*.

B + I Strategy (2012), *Estudio del Impacto Económico generado por la actividad del Museo Guggenheim Bilbao – Estimación a 2011*.

Da Silva Costa, J. (2013), *Impacto económico da Fundação de Serralves no âmbito do projeto improvisações/colaborações*. Fundação de Serralves and Porto Business School.

Department for Culture, Media and Sport, *Annual Report and Accounts 2016–17*.

Economic Development Research Group (2015), *Economic Impact Study of the Museum of Fine Arts*, Boston, MFA.

MFA (2017), *Museum of Fine Arts, Boston Strategic Plan*.

National Museums Liverpool, 2018, *NML consolidate statement of financial activities as at 31 March 2018*. National Museums Liverpool. p. 50.

Plaza, B. (1999), "The Guggenheim-Bilbao Museum effect: A reply to Maria V. Gomez' 'Reflective images: The case of urban regeneration in Glasgow and Bilbao'", in *International Journal of Urban and Regional Research* 23 (3), 589–592.

Regeneris Consulting (2017), *The Economic and Social Contribution of National Museums Liverpool*.

Rossi, G. (2014), "Tra cantieri e spese legali una grandeur da 130 milioni", ne *L'Alto Adige* del 19 marzo 2014.

Schneider, F., Dreer, E. (2015), "Wirtschaftsfaktor Therme Meran", Johannes Kepler Universität Linz, *Abgeschlossene Studien*, pp. 14–18.

Terme Merano Spa (2018), *Reports and financial statements as of 31.12.2017*.

Vicario (2017), *Is the Bilbao effect over?*, in "Apollo", March 2017.

Index

Note: Page numbers in *italics* indicate figures and those in **bold** indicate tables on the corresponding pages.

Printed in the United States
by Baker & Taylor Publisher Services